POOR IN SPIRIT

POOR IN SPIRIT

Awaiting All From God

Gabriel-Marie Cardinal Garrone

LIVING FLAME PRESS
LOCUST VALLEY, N.Y. 11560

Cover: Robert Manning

Copyright 1975 Darton, Longman and Todd, Ltd.

Published by Living Flame Press, Locust Valley, New York 11560.

Originally published as
Ce Que Croyait Jeanne Jugan
by Maison Mame, Paris.

ISBN 0232-51337-6

Printed in the United States of America.

CONTENTS

INTRODUCTION

Poor in spirit. . . .

What does this mean? How and why was Jeanne Jugan poor in spirit?

Something to do with her faith? — With that great and fundamental Christian reality: faith.

What then did Jeanne Jugan believe? What was her faith? I do not think that we shall find the answer by asking her just to run over her creed or her catechism. Her unity and simplicity of soul are so remarkable that, truly to respect them, we must go deeper, to the root of things. To faith — yes, of course — but to faith understood in its absolute and quintessential sense of abandonment to God, of unreserved acceptance of God's mind and will.

But, when we investigate this privileged soul, we make an extraordinary discovery: her faith, when seen like this, is indistinguishable from poverty! There is no better word than this for defining Jeanne Jugan's spirituality, irradiating her entire existence, giving a unique and original quality to every aspect of her life.

At a level as profound as this, the Lord's words

in the Gospel about poverty take on their fullest meaning. Only at a level as deep as this can we understand why the Lord accorded poverty the primacy among the Beatitudes, to which the Gospel invites us.

Poverty, of course, with regard to material possessions, as St. Luke understands it; poverty in the wider sense of humility, as St. Matthew explains it: but a poverty which in either case is first and foremost a confident and filial dependence on God, a total entrusting of oneself into his hands, with all that such a disposition engenders of peace, joy, wisdom, courage . . . all those good things in fact which St. Paul calls "the fruit of the Spirit" and which demonstrate that, in the ultimate analysis, faith, poverty and charity are one and indivisible.

There is, therefore, no reason to be surprised if, in this book on Jeanne Jugan's spirituality, you find much about poverty and indeed find yourself being led step by step to penetrate the many aspects of this virtue. For this is the only true and honest way of investigating her faith. And it is the only way, if we are not ourselves to forgo the benefit of having our own faith made more radiant by hers, the benefit of acquiring a heightened perception — yes, an unexpected one, too — of poverty, to which so many souls aspire without always knowing, today scarcely ever knowing, where its true source and its true nature lie.

That said, who am I of all people to make bold to undertake this book?

I can think of a number of reasons why I should not do so. Has not Monsignor Francis Trochu already written the last word on everything to do with Jeanne Jugan's life and work?

And yet, in the back of my mind, I am constantly aware of all the old people in the world; though their numbers are ever increasing in our society, their joy is not increased thereby. And, as against this, I often think of that house in Toulouse, marvellously clean and radiantly peaceful, where everybody's face beamed with joy; and I think too of the Little Sisters, gentle and attentive, to whom no need, no call, passed unregarded.

So, Little Sisters of the Poor, I write these pages deserving of greater talent and more love, to thank you on behalf of the aged poor whom you serve: and indeed on behalf of us all.

In some generous heart, perhaps the name and life of Jeanne Jugan will excite the questioning reaction: If it really is possible to sow joy in a huge sector of the world where irremediable sadness threatens to darken all, if it really is possible to contribute directly and personally to this miracle, why shouldn't I . . . ? How much more valuable that would be than all the vain, uncoordinated outpourings of love, whether real or promised, in the world today!

To someone reading this, perhaps Jeanne Jugan will reveal the secret of that love of which no particle is ever wasted — the love that begins and ends in poverty, true poverty which most people prefer to discuss rather than to live, and which they never achieve since the true source and meaning of poverty are to be found in God alone.

Little Sisters, poverty is your glory.

You work so that, for others, poverty may not be suffering, or at least not fruitless, unrewarded suffering. And you do this at the cost of being poor yourselves, like the Lord Jesus who "became poor to enrich us by his poverty."

Feast of the Poor Man of Assisi,
4 October 1974.

Note. This work in no way anticipates the judgment of the Church as regards the "sanctity" of Mary of the Cross, and the author submits absolutely to the authority of the Church in this matter.

A LIFE SURVEYED

A LIFE SURVEYED

The Little Sisters of the Poor are to be found all over the world.

Wherever there are men and women experiencing the cruel ordeal of old age with no one to love them, there you will find the Little Sisters of the Poor, to make sure that the aged do feel loved, to console those tired old eyes with an answering glance of affection, to love the aged poor as individuals.

The Little Sisters do this, and do it without fuss, almost without knowing, and have been doing so for more than a century in every corner of the globe.

In Brittany, where the Sisters first came into being, they are known as the "Jeanne Jugans," from the name, naturally enough, of the woman who was their foundress. And such a title was never so well deserved, since the humble woman who started the Little Sisters really did conceive, intend and achieve all that the Sisters should be and that they have now become. Without her, there would have been nothing. And the Little Sisters know that they will only continue to exist on condition that they are like her.

Foundress Jeanne Jugan certainly was the first mother of the Little Sisters. But never did foundation less resemble some grandiose project conceived by a powerful mind and gradually realized with resources previously accumulated. Far from it. And as for planning, the word barely applies, unless by it we mean a firm will, a lively awareness of the good to be done and an imperturbable trust in God's power to accomplish it.

And this aside, her act of creativity is more than ever remarkable, when viewed in superficial and purely human terms, since on the face of it all this foundress's activities are crowded into the space of three or four years. For those few years, she is and does everything. Everything begins with and from her: not only the first foundation, but those immediately born from it, further and further away. If a foundation begins to wilt, Jeanne Jugan is sent, Jeanne Jugan rushes to the rescue. She is the one to whom everyone turns; she is the one whom the public know and admire. But soon, her true role stops being an official one. And then, suddenly, she disappears. For the remaining quarter of a century of her life, she is nothing to anyone, not even to her own congregation. Miraculously forgotten, you might say. Only, present still like a shadow, like a witness, beside the Little Sisters studying in the Novitiate. Forgotten for a quarter of a century, though not by God who sees and knows all mysteries.

Deeper and deeper down the foundress dug to lay the first, humble foundation stone — herself — so that the edifice might rise all the higher. Without her, there would have been no Little Sisters of the Poor. And without fidelity to her example, they will come to an end.

Isn't this reason enough for describing and learning about this pure and noble character?

This book is not, and is not meant to be, a biography. It will draw without scruple on works and studies already in print,* although only to trace the impressively consistent course of Jeanne Jugan's existence. And this course, it seems to me, can best be summed up in a single sentence: Jeanne Jugan was one of the poor. And we say "one of the poor" as we might say "one of the saints."

Once we say this of her, the details of her life immediately seem to jump into a coherent pattern, just as a certain note will bring birds flocking from all points of the compass, just as a detail noted in a landscape or in a picture, a touch of colour observed by the eye of a Rembrandt or a Dickens, suddenly gives the key to the whole composition.

But this is conditional — as I shall try to show — on our agreeing about what exactly is meant by being poor. Jeanne Jugan did not force this on herself, she was it, just as Jesus did not waste time in telling us that he was our Saviour; he was it — which is better — and his deeds speak for him, the

*Notably *Une grande Bretonne, Jeanne Jugan*, Canon A. Helleu, Rennes 1938; *Jeanne Jugan*, Msgr. Francis Trochu, 2nd revised edition, 1960.

authority of his every word, the force of his slightest gesture. To some extent, we all tend to interpret spiritual truths to mean what we suppose will suit us best, thus falsifying and distorting the whole. If the brave title "one of the poor" is not to leave anything unsaid, is not to leave anything out of focus, we shall have to grasp things at the root, as Jeanne Jugan instinctively did, so reticently and discreetly. Not that she was secretive — but then neither was she talkative. The brave word "poor" had the same full meaning for her as it had for the Virgin Mary.

"Jeanne Jugan, one of the poor" then is to be our guideline, our viewing-point. But first we ought to run over the basic facts, various stages and salient events of her life, so that we can refer to them as we proceed.

There is thus no question of this being a biography, but rather a dictionary of the few geographical and historical landmarks needing to be known and sufficing to frame a life at once so simple and so rich. The few key-words of her vocabulary are not many, the same ones recur over and over again, as they do in the life of anyone poor. Jeanne Jugan's language is as poor as she is, and her sayings are correspondingly rare and brief: someone poor does not have time to talk, particularly when she is poor for other people's sake as well. Her horizon is narrow: poor people go on foot — which does not allow them to travel very far.

All this may sound very poor indeed, and poor indeed is the right word. There is, however, gran-

deur in all this, though of another order, like the
poverty of Christ. In the eyes of men, all this goes
for nothing; not so in the eyes of God, who (as
Pascal says) sees the wisdom of it — which later
bursts into sight for everyone. God is there with his
charity, giving new proportions to things. Jeanne
Jugan keeps her eyes lowered, she looks within, for
her the source of life is not among men. But when
she does raise her eyes, her face is radiant with
beauty. Young novices who knew her in her old
age still remembered that look with wonder when
they themselves were old — a look that had rested
on countless poor people's faces, leaving them in
turn radiant with a mysterious light, reaching down
into the depths of their hearts: the light of the love
of God.

Let us therefore say what little needs to be said,
making a brief inventory of places, dates and
names all quickly learnt, the better to go beyond
mere words and arrive at understanding.

We shall take a map of Brittany. Not of the whole
of France. One of Brittany will be quite enough.
Jeanne Jugan's travels barely took her out of this
area. Tours, where she went in response to a need,
is not very far away, nor is Angers. Before journey's end and her final twenty-five years of life,
God will have fixed his servant in this corner of the
world. At the last, she will only travel the way
from her cell to the chapel, from sewing-room to
garden.

I said: a map of Brittany. There are one or two
names on it that we ought to remember. But very,

very few. First, those that form the setting for her
beginnings: Cancale, Saint-Malo, Saint-Servan.
Then, those that mark the first — and for her, the
last — developments: Dinan, Rennes, distant Tours,
Angers. And that is the lot. Her whole life was to
be led within this narrow compass. She would have
been at home in a world as wide as this was narrow, had God so willed it, had he not asked her to
spend the rest of her days in obscurity, preparing
by sacrifice, prayer and penance, the resources
needed for the great expansion of the work which
others, not her, were to achieve. You see, had God
so willed, she could just as easily, perfectly and
efficiently have accomplished a more extensive
mission. But Jesus lived his life between Nazareth
and Jerusalem, today only a few hours away from
each other by car, and even in his time only a day
or two. But that was enough to save the world.
Jeanne Jugan's field of operations was no wider,
yet enough to fill the whole world with her daughters, enough to send them swarming into the four
corners of the globe.

Cancale: a picturesque Breton port near Saint-
Malo, where the fishing fleets regularly set out for
the long voyage to Newfoundland. Some men
come home again; others never do. The sea is
treacherous and implacable. Jeanne's father did not
come back. There, among the people you find a
general gravity, born of a constant awareness of the
possibility of death, of a father's non-return. Life is
serious, life is hard. People love each other more
for the fact of being separated and anxious
throughout their lives. People live closer to one

another in large families bereft of the one who by rights should be its moving spirit. People help one another. People know what it is to be needy, and indeed to be hungry. But life has to go on. Faith is their prop. Deep faith, somewhat severe too, in a world where every woman must be prepared to find herself widowed, if she is not already, and every child prepared to be orphaned. What is more, in Jeanne Jugan's case, this child came into the world during the convulsions of the French Revolution, at the height of the Terror. The first religious services she ever attended were held in secret. The first church that she was to see and go into, had been profaned again and again, then converted to secular uses. From the start, then, life had to be led with God within.

Such was the setting in which Jeanne Jugan served her apprenticeship for life, her heart the while growing humble, strong and deep. A little shepherdess leading the family's small flock of animals to pasture, and discovering the wondrous horizon of the sea, glittering into infinity. This impoverished existence, beset with anxiety over daily bread, the great peace of nature, and the enforced search for God in the recesses of her own soul, secretly prepared the firm will and pure heart which the Lord was later to need.

But life led between cottage and field, among little brother and sisters in a mother's wake, with the intermittent presence and soon the permanent absence of a father, was not to last. Jeanne was soon old enough to earn a little for the needy household. A job turned up. For several years,

Jeanne went into service with the Vicomtesse de la
Choüe whose estate lay near Cancale. After this,
she made an even more definite break with home:
she took a job at the hospital in Saint-Servan. A
first and painful act of detachment. She little realized that the humble ·drudgery of the hospital
would be the very experience on which grace
would seize to show her which way she must take.
She came to know the misery of the aged and,
simply and whole-heartedly, to love them. Nor was
she to lack that indispensable experience, only to
come once in her life, of being physically exhausted: God would need that too. To serve the
poor, he was preparing an instrument that would
never fail him. To understand the poor, Jeanne
Jugan had to know and to have lived something of
their own painful helplessness.

For God is working on her: this she knows. She
betrays as much in a characteristically brief confidence. She does not spend herself in effusions, not
even intimate ones. She has no time to study herself. But God, who speaks her own language and
who already rules her soul as Master, knows how to
make her understand. Jeanne at this stage knows
that "she will have a task to perform." She waits
for the Master to tell her more. But already she
knows enough, gently but firmly to discourage a
suitor, a sailor whose heart has been won by her
stout-heartedness and grace.

Her interior life is gradually taking shape. She
finds herself at home in the Third Order which,
two centuries earlier, one of Brittany's greatest
missioners, St. John Eudes, had bequeathed to the

ages as the durable fruit of his work for souls. In it, she learns to regulate her interior life, to spend lengthy periods in prayer to God, to God as revealed in the Heart of Jesus, hearth and source of love. More than a devotion, for her a profound commitment, a school in which the Heart of Mary is inseparable from the Heart of Jesus.

At Saint-Servan, she is led to organize her life in common with a friend who is older than herself. Everything, you may say, is now ready. The only thing needed is the spark to kindle a hearth never again to be extinguished. Jeanne already knows about the misery of old age. It only remains for her to realize its extent. She has made her heart available to the Lord, who now dwells in it and near whom she herself dwells; she has even had her first experience of the common life.

And then, one day, the Lord knocks at the door of the tiny flat where these two holy women are sharing their lives and their prayers. He asks for a place in their household: he finds it to his taste. How could anyone refuse? And this is how it all began. They moved up to make room for him, since that was what he wanted. They gave him the best place, of course. They did not know what this would lead to, but lead somewhere it certainly would and fast. The Lord was a poor old woman met by Jeanne: forsaken, without fire, food or shelter. Never mind! To be lovely and warm, in a comfortable bed, Jeanne's bed, with a bowl of soup and the priceless gift of a smile and friendship beyond the hope of dreams. The Lord was that poor woman. And the next one, and the next. The miracle has begun.

Hoisted up the narrow little stairs, where a rope serves for handrail, gradually invading what little space there is, the misery and old age of Saint-Servan take over the little bedroom as though they have a right to it. And soon it will be the loft as well, squeezing the two occupants before them. But the original occupants do not need beds any more, they have no time to think of themselves. If the old women are to be comfortable, they must come first. They are all-demanding: on time, on attention, on presence. . . . The Lord makes himself at home, He has become Master of the house. The call is irresistible. Like the great sea-wind, the Lord flings wide the door which, for the first visitor, had only been held ajar. Oh yes, there are plenty of others: the streets of Saint-Servan are full of poor wretches who have given up hopes of getting anything from anybody. And now, they catch sight of someone coming towards them and — what a wonderful discovery! — realize that someone really loves them.

The two little rooms, which you can still go and see, obviously would not stretch to infinity. But how were they to refuse the old people who came to the door? Women widowed by the sea, their strength giving way in old age or already gone; sailors no longer able to earn their rigorous living, threatened by want, indigence and drink. These do not take long to hear the incredible news that there is the hope of a home. So they come. And he who sends his poor provides handsomely for their recep-

tion. Jeanne is his docile and efficient instrument.
From the overcrowded flat, they move forthwith
to ground-floor premises providentially made available: the "Big Downstairs" to use the words of the
story. In miraculous order and dazzling cleanliness,
improvised beds are lined up. There is soon such a
squash that eventually they have to take over most
of the buildings of a disused convent, to which
Jeanne does not hesitate to make alterations and
additions; and this becomes their house.

Here, however, we must pause and go back a
little way. Physical expansion could not fail to
raise every kind of problem. First of all, staff; how
could Jeanne alone discharge the increasing house-
work? Spontaneously, around her the embryo of a
community begins to form. A problem of resources: "alms for the poor" starts being orga-
nized. God sends his friends, and God provides for
their needs. Those who tomorrow will be the
"Little Sisters of the Poor" and who today are
already servants of the poor, themselves do what
the poor do. Treading their pride underfoot, they
go with hand outstretched on behalf of the aged
poor, who can no longer do so for themselves.
They go collecting from door to door. God has
indeed prepared servants for his poor. Almost without meaning to, without realizing what lies in store
for them, three girls join Jeanne Jugan as helpers.
The task is so absorbing that they cannot stop;
they stay. Jeanne irradiates this first group with
her own intensity of life, her love for Christ and his
Mother, her unconditional devotion to the aged
poor, the joyous rigour of an existence entirely

given, but ordered, regular, silent and modest withal. A religious community in anticipation, to which neither rule nor exercises are lacking; nor a head — Jeanne herself. The religious authorities, who have looked favourably on the work from the outset, soon come to have confidence in it, even delegating the services of a young and zealous priest, to help the little group in its early stages as a community. Unfortunately, M. Le Pailleur was not as balanced a man as he was zealous. Though he served them well, his imagination gradually ran away with him; spurred by a vanity of which he was possibly even unaware, he assumed command. The work was his. He was, we shall soon hear, himself the founder, first conceiving, then willing and finally carrying it out. He was the one who had met the first poor woman. And he was the one who, by a concatenation of events, had gradually performed the miracle.

Lock, stock and barrel, M. Le Pailleur takes over the past. Initially without even realizing. But what he imagines and evidently ends by believing, he says and later puts into writing. He is the Founder, the Father. He will be the Superior. For Jeanne is not the woman to insist on her rights, or to pro-test. If he elbows her aside so that he can install a candidate of his own choice, one of his own peni-tents, as ruler of the little community, Jeanne is not the person to raise objections. She will obey . . . and we shall then see the extraordinary state of affairs where the foundress universally recognized as such and soon brought into the public eye as the recipient of a quite unexpected national award, and so famous even abroad that foreigners come specially to see her, is simultaneously pushed into the background within her own community, one humble servant among many others, condemned to obscure tasks and only called back to light when a foundation is on the verge of collapse, which by her reputation and personal gifts she instantly and miraculously restores to health. Then follows total obscurity. For twenty-seven years, Jeanne Jugan is one Little Sister doing her work in silence and self-effacement, providentially in contact with the novices of the community, on whom her example and discreet advice are quietly impressed, as these novices years later will bear witness.

Meanwhile a complete religious institution has sprung into being. Statutes codify experience and guarantee fidelity to its aims by laying down tried and certain means. The various influences may be detected here of direct experience, of the rule of St. John Eudes' Third Order, from which Jeanne drew her first impetus, and principally of the wise advice of the Brothers of St. John of God, whose mission was related to that of the Little Sisters and who, as well as helping, contributed something specifically theirs: the fourth vow of hospitality, that supremely heroic form of abandonment to the Lord. And thus Jeanne Jugan becomes Sister Mary of the Cross and signs community documents, when by chance anyone bothers to consult the foundress. The work is God's. Its Founder is he. He knows who is truly his, and of the first of these he demands that supreme collaboration: that of a humbled heart.

For what we intend, the essentials have now been stated. The thread of this simple life has now been spun. It only remains to let the shuttle run and we shall see the whole of Jeanne Jugan's life appear in fine and regular design, the law and secret of which is none other than poverty. To our own generation, so deeply and evidently moved by grace to seek a deeper poverty than before, Mary of the Cross has something to say. She knows what it means to be poor, to be really and truly poor. A love like hers is beyond criticism. Against it, as St. Paul says, there is no law. Anyone whose soul is healthy cannot but capitulate before it. How can we deny ourselves this beneficial, purifying, stimulating bath to find the true meaning of the grace of poverty, urging us to go beyond words and petty injustices, in short to make our soul most truly poor and thus to win that supreme blessedness promised and accorded by the Lord?

Jeanne Jugan, Mary of the Cross, one of Jesus Christ's true poor, we follow where you lead on your collecting round, telling your beads, putting your overloaded basket down from time to time to draw your breath, sometimes roughly brushed aside like an importunate beggar, yet through your daughters, day after day for a century and a half, you draw into your empty hands what the Father provides for his friends, the poor.

POVERTY

TRUE POVERTY

Having nothing of one's own. Awaiting all from God."

The religious career of Jeanne Jugan would appear, on the face of it, to be very different from that of St. Thérèse of Lisieux. In the case of the latter, whose life was brief and soon extinguished between the four walls of a cloister, it seems so desperately poor in events that the least detail, the slightest element, assumes astonishing importance. The riches of St. Thérèse's life are so interior that we should know virtually nothing about them, had she not, under obedience, day by day revealed her soul to us. Her life went by without notable movement or incident. Rich it is, nonetheless: a treasury of confidences, of thoughts, of notes barely all catalogued yet, constituting an inexhaustible mine of inspiration.

The life of Mary of the Cross, however, simple as it was, was not without vigorous contrasts. We can trace her course as she moves from place to place, as she meets new people, as her creation grows between her hands, until she enters that deep and final silence which, putting an end to her activities, throws them into vivid relief. In her case, on the other hand, she left none of the copious reflections that we might wish to have. Rare and brief remarks fixed in somebody's mind, simple pieces of advice — and these always the same — given to novices whose ways happened to cross hers. Mary of the Cross was not a writer. Not that she did not have plenty of things to write about; but she had other things to do than talking or writing. These were not her grace, nor to her taste.

All we have left to go on, then, are a few chance remarks, now collected into a thin but very charming volume called *Sayings of Jeanne Jugan* and linked together by a short but lively commentary. The editor of the book, a Little Sister, has delightfully conjured up the reactions that these brief sayings, entirely unliterary, so unaffected, so absolutely direct and even, apparently, banal, aroused in their first hearers. Most readers' reactions, I think, will be the same. Not that Jeanne Jugan was by nature secretive or unwilling to communicate with other people. This would have been completely at odds with her basic sense of apostolate. But she said what she said, as she should and could say it. And that was all she had to say. That was the person she was. And that was how she thought Little Sisters should be. Again, even in this, Jeanne Jugan was poor. But in this poverty, what riches! Here, nothing was less like absence of thought or of feeling. If anything, more like the pregnant sayings in the Gospel, clear and simple, flooding the receptive heart and soul with light.

And so it is that, in three short phrases, she managed to define the sort of poverty that was her life: "It is so beautiful to be poor, to own nothing, to await all from God!"[1]

You could never define poverty better. You could never define it any other way. No one who has not discovered this, can know what evangelical poverty means: that poverty which alone can win the promises for this life and for the life to come. This is not Mary of the Cross's particular version of poverty, but poverty in a nutshell, the very essence of poverty perfectly expressed with a sense of joyful wonder always and irresistibly associated with it: "How beautiful it is to be poor!"

So, to be poor means to have nothing. Primarily that and totally that. Poverty is an absolute.

Yet this absolute penury means nothing, has neither value nor virtue, unless it is the obverse, as it were, of an absolute abandonment to the goodness of God, unless it is an expression of this abandonment here and now among the things of this world. Someone poor is not merely someone who owns nothing, but someone who puts trust in God alone.

This way of understanding poverty is what we find, expressed more elaborately perhaps, but lived in exactly the same way, in a Thérèse of the Child Jesus, or indeed in a Francis of Assisi or a Vincent de Paul. For there is no other sort of Christian poverty. It is easy to see the relationship between

[1] Canon Helleu, *op. cit.*, p. 148.

Jeanne Jugan's little phrase and the wonderful compositions of St. Thérèse, indeed the identity of inspiration leaps from the page: "To recognize one's own nothingness, to await all from God, as a little child awaits all from its father. . . . Not to worry about anything, not to acquire possessions. . . . " And our thoughts may move on to the scene when St. Francis, having handed his elegant clothes back to his father, takes refuge naked under the bishop's cloak, happy now "only to have one Father, the One who is in Heaven," and henceforth to rely for sustenance on him who leaves no single bird of the heavens unfed.

"To own nothing and to await all from God." How disarmingly simple and yet how disarmingly full! The words sum up all that poverty can be. Without research, without recourse to books, Jeanne Jugan precisely states the very essence of all Christian poverty. This is precisely what gives poverty the right to call itself Christian; without this, it can never in honesty bear the name.

It should therefore be immediately clear that the fundamental characteristic, the spring, as it were, the heart of poverty is the fact of "casting oneself" on the Lord as Scripture says, of "trusting" God the Heavenly Father once and for all to sustain our lives and give us our daily bread, and of consenting to our life's being uniquely dependent on him. And this implies two things which we must now consider in some detail: the attitude towards God, which this total abandonment entails; and the attitude towards things, automatically requiring a radical and even, when grace is strong and the heart willing, an absolute detachment from them.

The resignation of oneself into the hands of God
is obviously not what most people would regard as
the first, or principal, still less indispensable, aspect
of poverty. And this is clear enough from what
they say, or write, on the topic. When people, as
now, so imperiously demand it of the Church, this
is certainly not what they have in mind. To this
crucial aspect, they are completely indifferent.
Either they think of poverty as material deprivation or, if any motive for this is envisaged, they
talk of love: love for the poor, love for Christ. To
be poor is to want to be detached from one's possessions; to want to identify with the poor in the
life they live and to want to imitate Christ in love.

Admittedly, neither of these notions is false. But
where people go wrong is in ignoring the essential
quality of poverty, which consists in "finding God
enough" for our life, in trusting him to support us,
in refusing to rely on material things for the props
that they are naturally supposed to afford us; it
means making God the sure foundation which we
need if we are to keep our balance and make pro-
gress along the road of life. Such an attitude, it
must be obvious, cannot be maintained without
some real privation, whether occasional or permanent, whether partial or absolute. It is hard to
imagine how poverty can be sincere if no oppor-
tunity is ever taken of putting it into effect, be it
that grace invites or that disposition itself impels.
Clearly too, abandonment to God for our means of
subsistence is one of the deepest, most delicate
expressions of a true love for God. At what other

time and in what other way shall we be most truly
children of God, can we most truly call him by his
rightful name of Father, than at that moment
when we consent to risk everything in absolute
reliance on him; when we believe so firmly in his
love that we abandon *terra firma* and cast off into
the unknown, confident that the hand of God will
sustain us? Whoever then talks of poverty, talks in
some degree about privation. Whoever talks about
poverty in the Christian sense, talks in some degree
about love. But the essential thing about poverty
does not lie even in real material deprivation. Hear
what St. Paul says: his brand of poverty consists in
"knowing how to abound" as well as in "knowing
how to lack"; the essence of poverty does not lie in
loving, though loving is what inspires it and forms
its basis, but in the act of "faith," in the grand
biblical sense, in the fatherhood of God as sufficient for sustaining our existence.

Now, what St. Thérèse of the Child Jesus has
received (the grace of being able so felicitously to
expound for us by recording her own very real
experience of poverty), Mary of the Cross for her
part has mutely lived — apart, that is, from telling
us the meaning of her behaviour in one marvellously concentrated formula: "Having nothing, and
awaiting all from God." What St. Thérèse lives and
explains for the benefit of those whom she hopes
to attract into her "little way," Jeanne Jugan lives
without explanation, not hiding her secret but trying to attract rather by example than by words.

Jeanne progresses towards her Lord and towards

being like Christ, living for and by his Father. Each
step brings her nearer. But each step, by the same
token, requires a new wrench, though she never
betrays how great the inward wound. And each
step demands anew that act of faith in him who
can replace all human supports, "supported by no
support" as St. John of the Cross would put it.
Mary of the Cross exemplifies his poem in her life.
Wrenched from the loving, peaceful atmosphere of
home and family, for the loneliness and unfamiliar-
ity of life "in service." Torn from one settled and
regulated environment, for the experiences of a
new and unfamiliar one. Losing the pleasant relationship which she and her close friend Francoise
had begun to build between them. Then, knowing
the quiet regularity and simple joys of a humble
home for two, only to find herself suddenly
snatched out of this quiet existence and catapulted
into huge adventures which gradually deprive her
of her freedom, of her bed, of her independence
and even of the minutest of those possessions properly hers. From the moment that the first old
woman enters the attic, Jeanne knows that she no
longer owns herself and that she will never own
anything ever again. Every day anew, she has to set
off for some new, unknown goal, has anew to place
her faith in him who gives what he demands, but
who requires our faith and who withdraws one by
one the props of human security from us. All is to
be awaited from God alone. For Mary of the Cross,
this is no mere disposition of the heart, but a
necessity every minute of the day. She cannot take
one step concordant with the will of God as repre-

sented by these old people who keep arriving one after another, without in her heart knowing that wonderful sense of risk in resourceless abandonment to him who wants to be our all. Rather like a ship, affronting the high adventure of the seas and, from one wave to the next, throwing overboard the equipment designed to safeguard it in wind and storm. In the end, there is nothing left to jettison: the ship is now no more than an empty shell at the mercy of the elements. Will it sail on? Will it capsize and sink? And all we are left with is an aged Little Sister who has succeeded in dying without any personal possessions other than the little crucifix of a professed nun, one day to be recovered from her coffin. What numberless acts of faith and love passed to God through that lowly scrap of metal, worn by her lips and eaten away by time.

Mary of the Cross's departure made no stir on earth, left no empty place in the house. She had nothing left but God, which is to say All.

In that work of loving faith called poverty is a radical summons to absolute deprivation. Given that real deprivation depends on the dictates of circumstance and of God's will freely operating on the individual soul, it follows that no one can be a Christian without consenting deep down in his or her heart to a deprivation virtually without limit: that very deprivation dependent on a right notion of God and of the faith which God's fatherhood deserves from us, that very deprivation demanded by Christ when, addressing his future disciples, he gave them the list of things that they would have to abandon if they were to follow him. It would be going beyond God's wishes, if we were to impose deprivation on other people, since Providence alone, as regards each individual, decides the degree of deprivation suitable for each; but it would be morally wrong to encourage any Christian to imagine that his faith will not one day demand such a sacrifice of him, or not to suppose that he ought, deep down in his heart, not to prepare himself for meeting this demand.

Basically and by intention, Christian poverty cannot be other than absolute, comprising all things present and to come.

And hence it happens that, as a direct mark of love, God will ask one or another of his servants to perform and put into practice what that servant, as a Christian, has already in theory consented to do. He summons faith and love to prove themselves by boldly choosing God instead of those earthly things within our reach on which we normally rely for support as substitutes for God; to trust to God that we shall not die when the bread runs short; to look peacefully to the Lord when our hands are empty of those essentials that he gives us day by day and without which we cannot survive.

Thus, Jeanne Jugan tells us how far we must be willing to go, were it so to please God to ask us. She shows us what lies at the root of our faith, and of all faith; what it really means to call God our Father. Jeanne's poverty in everything about her shows us the depths of our own heart, the sort of God we have and what it means to be one of his children. When God does not seem to be asking for anything, we run a serious risk of living our lives as though the goods which we hold from God, and which are the proximate instruments of his providence, are more necessary and more precious to us than God himself — as though they were there to fill the gap, should God happen to forget about us. Happy indeed, then, the man or woman of whom grace demands real deprivation! How easy it is to understand Jeanne Jugan's deep joy in living a deprivation of this kind! The indescribable joy of depending only on God, of leaning only on him, "of eating from his hand," of calling him "Father"! "How beautiful it is to be poor!" How can we fail to understand that cry, or the faith from which it springs?

"Our Lord was poor," Jeanne Jugan said, "and I too want to stay poor until I die."[2]

"Poverty is my treasure."[3]

"Oh, if we only understood what riches we are heaping up for heaven, how we should love our poor mended clothes and our poor food!"[4]

"Once you go to a house, be poor, stay poor in everything."[5]

"If you want to please God, you must love poverty."[6]

How far away we are here from the partial and materialistic ideas commonly held about poverty!

[2] Reported by Sr. Céline de l'Ascension (Fanny Duchamp).
[3] *Ibid.*
[4] Reported by Sr. Arsene de Saint-Jean (Blandine Leydet).
[5] Reported by Sr. Céline de l'Ascension.
[6] Reported by Sr. Anne de Sainte-Marie (Juliette Gicquel).

For that is often the very reverse of true poverty,
resembling it about as much as the back of a tap-
estry resembles the front. That kind, seen from the
human point of view, is merely a wrench, merely a
privation, merely a kind of dismemberment, leaving us to a greater or lesser degree mutilated and
suffering. But true poverty must be first and foremost looked at from the point of view of God, as
an act of faith and love by very nature limitless.
God seems to deprive Jeanne Jugan, Mary of the
Cross, bit by bit of all her poor possessions. Each
step, she has to repeat her act of abandonment
which, being her true wealth, puts her so to speak
in possession of God. The simple, well-found comfort of which the old woman deprived her by taking her bedroom and her bed, by eating the last
piece of bread left in the house: this sort of comfort Jeanne will never know again. Far from it: day
by day, right to the end, she will learn that there is
always something more to be given even when
there is nothing left. And another comfort takes
the place of the former, another joy.... "Love
poverty!" she would repeat to the novices. "Poor
as we were, we were happy."[7]

Christian poverty concerns both man and God.
And in principle, it tolerates no limits.

Only circumstances and the will of God can say
what degree this deepest form of poverty — this
soul of poverty woven of faith and love — shall
take as regards material privation. And privation is
the only visible sign of what is within.

[7] Reported by Sr. Anatolie du Saint-Sacrement (Marie-Francoise
Dauphin).

POOR AMONG THE POOR

It is not possible for true poverty not to feel the need, or not to find the occasion, for manifesting itself to the world.

And this almost always happens in contact with the poor.

Someone poor is someone who is in need. That is, someone who, perhaps even without realizing, is calling to God for help. And God then draws him or her to the attention of one of his servants, who then becomes the instrument of God's compassion. This is the poor man's "neighbour," his brother in God's name. Christ loved the poor. He came to bring them the incredible good tidings that they were not rejected and forsaken. A sudden voice summons them from their loneliness. Unlikely as it may seem to them, the poor suddenly realize that they are loved, that someone knows who they are and calls them by name. Jesus is calling them, God is calling them. And, on God's behalf, one of God's friends is calling them.

God indeed was first in making himself poor, the better to be near and to give an example to his

servants. He did not care to have so much as a
stone on which to rest his head. He had no roof of
his own. He went without what nature affords even
to birds and creatures of the wild, be it nest or lair.
He was even ready to let himself be stripped of his
clothes, for his tunic to be thrown to and diced for
by the soldiers. Naked he went up, to die on the
cross.

Thus, every poor man henceforth will see himself in his God, and everyone can recognize God in
each poor man. "I was naked," he will say on Judgment Day, "I was sick, I had no clothes, I was
alone. . . . " He was himself the poor, in whom
God's friends would recognize him to their eternal
joy, and in whom others would despise him to
their own damnation. When someone, whom faith
awakens to the radical kind of poverty of which we
have been speaking, meets dynamic poverty in the
person of his God, the illumination ensuing is irresistible, whether like the dawn it takes the form of
gentle but instant impulsion, or like a thunderbolt
it detonates in the depths of the soul. In either
case, the grace is the same. There is no intrinsic
difference between the light which gently takes
possession of Jeanne Jugan's soul, and that which
on the instant seized the soul of Father Chevrier*
at his Christmas meditation before the crib.

There are all sorts of ways, some barely and
some not at all Christian, in which we may
"encounter" poverty. But in the ultimate analysis,

*Blessed Antoine Chevrier (1826-1879) was a French priest who
founded the Institut du Prado at Lyon, in 1860.

that encounter only merits the name, once we discover that Jesus and the poor are identical, that
poverty coincides with God in Christ.

Father Chevrier was gazing at the Infant Jesus
one Christmas evening. That was when everything
began for him. Later, he used to encourage his own
disciples to meditate long on that same mystery at
the crib. For him, as for them, this was the source
of his love for the poor, and of his decision to
become one of them to serve them. People have
tried to explain this sudden, decisive experience as
being his tardy discovery of poverty as human,
sociological fact, an exceptionally acute apprehen-
sion of the poverty in the world and of the poor
man's lot in modern society. But this is to put a
humanistic interpretation on an event of an entirely different order. What gripped and overwhelmed
Fr. Chevrier's heart once and for all was the poverty of his God — God's poverty as reflected by all
those poverty-lined faces, God's poverty, making
this priest for ever a servant of the poor. Throughout his life, the theme of Fr. Chevrier's ardent contemplation was to be the poor man Jesus Christ.
All his teaching tirelessly repeated and embroid-
ered on the lesson: "How wonderful Jesus Christ
is!" — words that he would repeat over and over
again in an ecstasy of admiration. "How beautiful
it is to be poor," Jeanne Jugan used to say. The
same tone of voice: the same light, drawn from the
same source.

In a flash, Father Chevrier discovered the identity of God and poverty in the Christ Child's
cradle. With no sudden revelation, Jeanne Jugan

recognized the image of her God, already entirely occupying her heart, in the poor, resourceless, fireless woman. "He has come!" Her faith is alert and deep enough for the recognition to be instantaneous, without external commotion or blinding light, and for the recognition to be instantaneously translated into action. She takes the old woman in her strong arms, brings her into her house and sits her down in her own chair. "Tonight, I am coming to stay with you." Jeanne's heart was ready. The only thing lacking was the actual encounter, to turn this attentive faith into the dynamism of incredibly fruitful activity. The fire was alight, the flame of faith was there, vigorous and bright. The flame encountered the first piece of kindling, fastened on it and, lo and behold! the whole house was ablaze!

Thenceforth, with mounting astonishment and admiration, we watch the effects of this first action reverberate throughout her life, and on beyond it. Ceaselessly we hear Jeanne Jugan repeating the same simple thing to her daughters, the same simple message of faith, determining the decision made and motivating the life led by a Little Sister of the Poor. On her lips, the words hardly ever change. It would be a waste of time to say more. And what would be the point in any case? What could lectures and elaborations add? Only the light that comes from on high can reveal and convince of this wonderful identity of God with the poor. The point is, that this light should enlighten us and that we should immediately act on the discovery thus made. Then the light will never go out.

"Little ones, never forget that the poor man is

our Lord himself."[1]

"Love, have great respect for the poor, always see God in them. You must never make them unhappy. You must always see our Lord in the poor."[2]

"Once you go to a house, be kind to the aged, particularly to the infirm. Love them sincerely . . . Yes, be kind."[3]

We could go on repeating the same simple phrase indefinitely. How often the young novices heard it! The novice who used to bring the aged Little Sister Jeanne Jugan her daily bread; the one who used to give her a hand for the hard climb up the main stairway; the one who asked her advice in the corridor; the novices assembled in the recreation room for spiritual reading, interrupted from time to time by terse little comments. Their witness is impressive: not one of them, years later, displays other than gratitude for this monotonous reminder, lodged in their minds for the rest of their lives and recalled long afterwards in answer to those taking evidence in Jeanne's process for Beatification.

And this was really the key to their own vocation. St. John does not bore us or weary us when, in his Epistle, as also (we can tell), to his disciples, he repeats over and over again that we must love one another and that there is no other law but this. Mary of the Cross talks the same language: "Treat

---

[1] Reported by Sr. Léontine de la Nativité (Marie-Joséphine Barbier).

[2] Reported by Sr. Christine de la Providence (Modeste Gerbaud).

[3] Reported by Sr. Saint-Aurélien (Marie-Ange Gautier).

the poor compassionately, and Jesus will treat you kindly. All your life to your dying day, you will be blessed, and you will always be able to run to him in your difficulties and troubles."[4] "Really love the poor, really take care of them — they are our treasures."[5]

Jeanne Jugan really became, in Christ, poor among the poor. People could not tell the difference between her and them, and this was supreme joy to her.

"Get into line! Like the others!" the town hall official at Saint-Servan shouted at Jeanne Jugan when she humbly came to collect her share of the dole for the aged poor in her house. In this man's eyes, she was not there "for them," she was "one of them." We ought to be grateful to him for having said this. Unintentionally, he gave the supreme accolade to someone who had identified herself with the poor, with whom Jesus too had identified himself. The blow was a humiliation to the collecting sister Jeanne Jugan, but must have filled her heart with joy untold.

Jeanne was truly poor among the poor.

Identified with them, that is to say, with her Lord.

---

[4] Reported by Sr. Marie de Saint-Romain (Marie-Rosalie Imbert).

[5] Reported by Sr. Marie de Saint-Thomas (Elizabeth McNamara).

POOR FOR THE POOR

And that was how Jeanne Jugan won the freedom of the City of the Poor.

But, as for the great sovereign Poor Man, this freedom, acquired by love, confers only the privilege of serving. Among the poor, Jeanne is their servant. Her humility is not inertia but activity; it is a spring stretching her soul to its utmost possible degree of expansion, so that she can cooperate with Christ for the good and salvation of the poor, from whom she herself is indistinguishable.

Every Little Sister will be a servant of the poor.

Christian intuition has never thought of poverty as a purely personal quality, as a sort of paradoxical riches to be hoarded for ourselves. This sort of poverty, stoical and pharisaic, has little in common with the poverty of Jesus. We should be back again among the wealthy, and even among the most dangerously wealthy of them: those who possess spiritual riches, noble wealth less willingly renounced and more inclined than any to delude and lead us astray from our goal. Jeanne Jugan was not only poor among the poor, she was poor for their sake.

The poor have nothing, they ask from those who have, they hold out their hands, they beg. Jeanne Jugan had not foreseen this: the old women whom she took in, still had to go begging their bread if they wanted to eat. Jeanne did not hesitate: she went instead of them. Off she went, collecting! Instead of the old women going begging, she went on their behalf. "Collecting" sounds a rather refined activity, but the reality of it is not. And we can sympathize with the feeling of the girl recruited by Jeanne and anxious to follow her, when she had to take her basket and set out. We can sympathize with the feelings of her family at the idea of their daughter going out begging like an old woman on behalf of old women.

Among the sayings of Jeanne Jugan still preserved, there are many to do with collecting: "Be careful not to rush your collecting and not to blurt out what you want as soon as you open your mouth, as though you were owed it. Take time to say good morning and, if appropriate, to say a few words to show your interest in the people themselves and in what is going on. This is more little, and less pressing. Then gently explain the needs of the house, but do not be wearisome."[1]

"Do not ask for something as though you were owed it" . . . "a few words" . . . "This is more little" . . . "do not be wearisome" . . . What depth in this advice! What wisdom! — that was the very word Jeanne would use, in urging her daughters to pray for success in discharging their difficult task.

---

[1] Reported by Sr. Isabelle de Saint-Paul (Claudine Jonin).

Mary, Mother of Wisdom, is the one whom she likes to invoke: "You will need all the wisdom you can have, when you are collecting sisters."[2]

The humility is not put on. It is not tactical: "Recollection, proper posture, politeness, taking care to shut people's doors quietly; out of doors, the habit of telling your beads, hiding them under your cloak, to avoid strictures from people who do not understand what we are."[3] To behave "without fuss" . . . "with littleness." That is true poverty speaking. But are we really talking about poverty, or about charity? We seem to be very near St. Paul, as he writes of the "greatest of the gifts" of the Lord.

Humility, yes, but certainly patience too, in all its rigour and in all its forms: patience which again St. Paul puts right at the top of his list of charity's attributes. The patience needed for walking in the cold, along muddy roads, without losing heart, with a heavy basket on your arm. Patience to bear the affront of harsh words, of doors slammed irritably in the collector's face, of the gift ungraciously given. The memory is preserved of a blow with which a bad-tempered old man once emphasized his refusal. Also preserved is Jeanne's stoical answer: "That was for me, Sir . . . now please give me something for my poor."[4]

Perseverance too: with friends often tired of

[2] Reported by Sr. Valentine Joseph (Marie-Joseph Robert).

[3] Reported by Sr. Sainte-Amélie (Jeanne-Marie Chabrier).

[4] Reported by Sr. Anne Auguste (Adélaïde Désert) and Sr. Saint-Albert (Elisabeth Carrausse).

being asked, Jeanne was not afraid of gently per-
sisting. Patience is not a passive virtue: "I shall not
go away until you have given me a few potatoes
and crusts, for me to make our old people's
soup."[5] Differently expressed and with people well
disposed, her perseverance was the same: "You
gave me something yesterday? — But, Sir, my poor
were hungry yesterday, and now they are hungry
today, and tomorrow they will be hungry too."[6]
And here is another conversation still on record:

"Well, Jeanne, what are you doing here?"

"I am waiting, Sir."

"Is that all, Jeanne?"

"I am collecting for my women."

"Your women? I don't know why you've lum-
bered yourself with them. Are you trying to lum-
ber me with them too?"

"We shall share them between us today, Sir, if
you will be so kind. You will feed them and I shall
look after them. . . . Give me a nice lot and you
won't see me again for a long time . . . I shall pray
for you, Sir. They too will pray for their benefactor. I shall make sure that they are grateful."[7]

This was all conducted with such tact and perfect charity, that one witness has spoken of the
"supreme grace"[8] with which this collecting sister
did her job for God. She knew whom she was

---

[5] Letter of Mlle. Kervern, great-granddaughter of Admiral Tre-
houart de Beaulieu.

[6] Letter of Mme. E. de Molon.

[7] Mme. de la Corbinière, *Jeanne Jugan et les Petites Soeurs des
Pauvres*, Paris, Lecoffre, 1883, p. 170.

[8] Léon Aubineau, Introduction to Mme. de la Corbinière, *op. cit.*

working for; she knew that "God would bless" her work, and that the benefactors would be the first to benefit from it. And, in the same spirit, she used to speak about them to the novices, recommending them not only to promise to pray for them but actually to do so.

"Little ones, when you go out collecting, some people will behave charitably, and others will swear at you and send you packing. The neighbours will say: 'You had a very poor reception next door,' but you must never show resentment. When this happened to me, I used to say: 'Oh no, those people treated me very well.' For you see, little ones, when people are nasty to you, it is good for us and something we can offer to God."[9]

Collecting done in the spirit of Jeanne Jugan is a perfectly normal and direct response to a need. All the dissertations in the world are of no avail against want. There will always, alas, be old people in need, whom not all the institutions in the world will be able to reach. And even if, impossible though it is, the public authorities did manage to cater completely for all needs, why should private initiative, inspired by charity, not go on supplementing what no public authority however well intentioned can ever give: the basic assurance of friendship and of personal devotion inspired by friendship? I shall never forget an old woman coming to see me one day, to ask if she could be admitted to the local house run by the Little Sisters. I was surprised, knowing how well run the institu-

---

[9] Reported by Sr. Saint-Michel (Marie-Amélie Mouillot).

tion was where she was already living. What more
could she want? "To have someone to love me,"
was her straightforward answer. That more than
justifies Jeanne Jugan's original impulse.

POOR IN HEART

Many long-standing accusations are levelled against
Christian charity. One of the more specious of
these is that charity, where human beings are concerned, is not love really and truly sincere. For
charity — so people say — the poor are only the
pretexts for loving Someone Else. They are thus
only made use of. The Christian practicing charity
goes through the motions of love and friendship
with human beings, but his heart is fixed else-
where. Now, real love would not stoop to this cha-
rade: people need to be loved for themselves; the
attitude towards them that Christian charity
adopts is not good enough.

The argument is in fact too clever by half, since
the effects of Christian charity speak for themselves. The facts preclude valid objection. Were
anyone bold enough to challenge the value or reality of St. Vincent de Paul's love for "My Lords the
Poor," the poor, who are best judges in the case,
would be the last to dispute the value of the feelings and the devotion, the benefits of which they
themselves receive.

Nonetheless, the theoretical objection remains. And, if unresolved, it will slowly poison the spirit. Even if the argument is sophistical, it places an unhealthy germ of suspicion deep in the mind. And then it only needs the right occasion, for the germ to develop, giving birth to real doubts, which in turn produce real desolation. Yes, these occasions do occur: there is no shortage — and indeed there never has been — of Christian "do-gooders" (the distasteful expression is well found) who give the beneficiary the sensation of being only the medium through whom and beyond whom the charitable intention passes. He is instantly aware of being wronged, he senses that he is being used, he does not feel loved.

That is the objection.

It ought to be immediately obvious that here we have an obfuscation, that this is nothing whatever to do with Christian charity. When the beneficiary is not truly loved for himself, the "someone else," love for whom he feels passing through him, is not in fact God, but egoism, convention. . . . Yes, ultimately a subtle form of egoism, not indeed necessarily conscious. But, be that as it may, the true God is not involved.

For the fact is that God is not "Someone Else," even if human language cannot do without this sort of expression; God is not to be reckoned among his creatures. He is the one who gives them in existence, and in him they find not only their earliest origin but also their supreme end. They only live by virtue of being part of him; they only move by virtue of seeking him, whether hesitantly or

directly, as their Supreme Good. A total dependence on God, a total desire to love him, are present in everyone, not as a supplementary ingredient
to be added to the love that we bestow on created
things that capture our attention, but as the
supreme reason for all influence and for all love.

Hence, when true and sincere, our love for God,
far from competing with human beings for a place
in the human heart, justifies our love for other
people and provides the impulse for it. We love in
God, when love deserves the name. Love for God
and love for other people are not opposed but
complementary, as are stream and spring, as are
reflection and sun. Hence, St. John the Apostle, in
his First Epistle, straightforwardly mixes love for
God and love for our brothers in a way which
makes nonsense of distinctions which we often like
to draw. Loving God makes for loving others, and
loving others is only pure and steadfast when loving God is its deep and conscious foundation. God
is not jealous of his creatures, he does not exploit
them in demanding our love, since he himself is the
essence of love and generosity.

And this is why no one loves as truly, no one
loves as unselfishly, no one loves with more abandonment, with more perseverance, with more generosity, than a true friend of God.

The first fruit and surest criterion of authentic
love for God is precisely that respect which he
inspires in us for those whom he makes us love.
Not only does he not reduce them to the ignoble
condition of being means and instrument to the
service of someone else, but he obliges us to

consider them first and foremost for what they themselves are, and to treat them as worthy of true consideration. Charity, far from being unaware of, or from overlooking, what is right and due, contrariwise insists on it as being of prime importance. Treating our neighbour for God's sake as intrinsically worthy of respect — this is what loving God imposes first and foremost on the Christian heart.

So it was neither by accident nor due to some surplus of perfection added to her charity, that Jeanne Jugan used to treat the aged with such exquisite tact. This has to be emphasized, before we see her in action. Her tact is not to be admired as an exceptional gift, but merely to be recognized as a sign of her true love for God, as the proof that God is truly loved, that God is truly present. Any other way of going about things, any element of negligence or carelessness would, by the same token, have been a bad mark, rightly giving scope for doubt about the quality of her love for God. Just so, St. Vincent also loved the poor and treated them as "lords," in the grand tradition codified in the rule of the medieval hospitallers in their hospitals: "Our Lords the Poor."

And now it is time to see how Mary of the Cross treated her old people. In her life so impregnated with charity, we see things as though bathed in a gentle, steady light. Rarely does a vivid flash allow us to pick out a detail. And what indeed can stand out where the days are all alike, where the gift which each Little Sister has made of herself is permanent and absolute, where care for the well-being and happiness of the aged absorbs everyone's time and attention?

For everything belongs to them. From what is collected, the best must be reserved for them. Never mind what is left for the Little Sisters. If there are only a few dry crusts left — as used to happen in the earlier foundations — they dip them in water and eat them with joy and gratitude. On one such occasion, Jeanne Jugan remarked: "For little beggar maids, anything should be tasty."[1]

Whatever the aged want, they must be given. Do not worry about yourself: God will provide. They come first. Let them be well served and be happy. "Forget about yourself" in serving them and leave the rest to God.

No attention is too great for those, of whom Jeanne told the Little Sisters: "God is doing you a great favour by calling you to serve him in the poor, for in serving them, you are serving him."[2]

Within each of the lively, good-hearted girls whom Jeanne sees coming and going about her for quarter of a century, she discerns the Little Sister who will finally emerge. She follows each with a loving yet pitiless eye. The depositions in Jeanne's process are unanimous — surprisingly so — in mentioning the inflexible firmness with which she would correct an attitude, a way of talking, of walking, anything that might later develop into carelessness, negligence or inattention as regards the aged.

Their rights were paramount.

[1] Reported by Sr. Pascaline (Marie-Louise Daniel).

[2] Reported by Sr. Marie de Saint-Romain.

"You make too much noise at your work and, once you go to a house, you will tire the poor sick people and cause them suffering."[3] Youth needs to let off steam. There would be nothing wrong with this if there were no aged to be considered and whom the commotion might distress.

"Whatever you are doing, little ones, make a habit of doing it well, so that later when you are working with the aged, you will be able to take care of them properly; for in them, you are caring for Jesus himself."[4]

"When you are with the aged, be kind, be very kind . . . be a mother to them."[5]

"When you are with the poor, give yourself with all your heart."[6]

Tirelessly, Jeanne intervenes. Tomorrow must be planned for. Little Sisters must learn to watch themselves, and to govern themselves entirely by the good and happiness of the men and women whom they will one day have the honour of serving.

Nothing is more telling than this insistence on self-control. Indulge the aged, never let them see a tense or indifferent face: "Our old folk do not like long faces."[7] For their sake we must always look bright "when things go wrong," in worries and

---

[3] Reported by Sr. Saint-Théotime (Jeanne-Marie Garin).

[4] Reported by Sr. Marie Lambertine (Reine Vilfeux).

[5] Reported by Sr. Marie de Saint-Romain.

[6] Reported by Sr. Séraphine du Saint-Esprit (Marie-Zélie Varinot).

[7] Reported by Sr. Noël-Joséphine (Marie-Joseph Aubry).

troubles, keep, as she would say, "looking cheerful."

All these simple things — not to mention the order and cleanliness so stringently required — say more eloquently than words what true charity means: loving. All are expressive of that forgetfulness of self demanded every minute by love. The solemn dissertations of remote pundits fade into insignificance before all this. Respect like this has nothing deceitful or deceptive about it. This is what loving really means. And this, a gift conferred by Jesus.

POOR IN WILL

The sense in which we have already used the terms
tact, respect and kindness to the poor, indicates
the sense, when speaking of Jeanne Jugan, in which
we shall interpret the word "heart." But this grand
Gospel word is so commonly abused that we ought
to spend a little while reconsidering it.

As Maurice Blondel remarks in one of his spiritual notes, the true name for the heart is will.
Nothing could be remoter from a facile and superficial sentimentalism than love for the poor as
evinced by Jeanne Jugan and the Little Sisters.
Nothing could be remoter from that type of "pity"
arousing a blind girl to such furious repugnance
that she recently wrote a devastating book called
Leur Sale Pitié (Their Foul Pity). Jeanne Jugan is
not a "bleeding heart." That sort of pity is alien to
her, her foundations are not laid on that: cut-price
pity, leaving the poor to their misery — only, a
little more aware of it than before, and hence that
much more miserable. Jeanne Jugan loves in a different way and her sort of love is at odds on every
score with the kind of pity which is a caricature of

love. Her heart is truly poor, poverty for her is not some rich woman's luxury. Superficial emotionalism is not for her; nor for true feeling, any of the innumerable substitutes produced by a combination of hypocrisy and vanity and venting themselves as often as not in hot air, tinted with righteous or scandalized indignation.

Jeanne Jugan's love, though charged with feeling, has its seat in the will. Not therefore love that talks, but love that acts. A love ever concentrated on its goal, never wasted on unproductive side issues. She loves, she holds her tongue, she acts, she utters no reproaches. Her heart is heavy with a love engendered by the will, under God.

Agreed, human pity is a good thing in itself. A man unmoved by the sight of suffering is a monster. But this is merely the reflex of a healthy spirit "still with something human about it." Devotion and love impervious to this natural emotion would be indeed inhuman, devoid of that element essential to the exercise of charity and making exchange and communication possible. But if we were to remain at this stage, we should not touch the true organ of charity: which is the will.

In Jeanne Jugan's love for the poor, we can easily recognize that truest form of love, the characteristics of which are described by St. Paul in terms most apt — be it said — for ridding us of the type of pity so prompt to move the heart, yet making no demand on it for action.

Jeanne Jugan's kind of love "seeks no return."

There is no real need to emphasize this. Her actions take place at a level and in a world both absolutely alien to any self-return. Collecting, from which her houses draw their sustenance, keeps her constantly in a state of humility. The admiring curiosity, which she from time to time arouses, finds her not so much embarrassed by it as impervious to it, and only anxious to be rid of these intrusions as fast as may be. If inner struggle she had, before she could accept insults and humiliations, that battle was soon won. If this still requires effort, this has become habitual to her, where humiliations are concerned. But as regards seeking or enjoying any personal satisfaction, this seems to have been entirely left out of her make up. Her type of activity is quite alien to this. People may honour her if they so please, when the good of her poor is involved, but, for herself, let them leave her alone.

What interests and preoccupies her is not herself, but God and his poor. And hence, her charity is not incensed by other people, in the more or less wicked way that ours is when the miseries of the poor incite us to pass an often outraged judgment on people who do not want to know and will not cooperate with us. Our charity all too frequently amounts merely to righteous indignation, by which we minister to our self-esteem at no cost to ourselves, and without the poor being any the better off. Hot air, that is all. But what a forceful example Jeanne Jugan sets us! We already know what she used to say to the novices and the sort of lessons she gave them, the humble, sisterly attitude they were to adopt towards people who shut the door in their faces or insulted them. She would not

tolerate that these should be judged, or even that
bystanders should be allowed to judge them. God
is the knower of secrets, God is the one who will
judge. For us to condemn them in defiance of the
Lord's will subtracts from the purity of our action,
and the victim of our shallow indignation is primarily us.

And so, consistent with many a Gospel precept,
Jeanne Jugan's charity is not one of words. She
wants her collecting sisters to say no more than
makes known the need. The Little Sister holds out
her hand, she explains why, she says thank you if
given reason to do so, she promises her prayers,
and goes her way, entirely turned towards the Lord
whom she will soon be meeting again in her "aged
poor," and with whom she continues her humble
interior conversation, her rosary being the simple
and appropriate means. Charity is not deceived,
and will not let verbal indignation take the place —
a very natural and dangerous temptation — of real
action, leaving us with the treacherous illusion of
having done our bit. How striking the contrast
between the speech maker hungry for·applause and
the humble woman moving on with a gentle bow.
Everyone sees and knows where the truth lies.

But charity's most dangerous enemy of all lies
within. Its name is sentimentality. It is easy to
attribute good motives to ourselves or to believe
that we have a sensitive conscience when our emotions are aroused. But the soul drowns, as it were,
in its own sensibilities. A "bleeding heart" is not
necessarily a charitable one. Jeanne Jugan does not
care for talk, she loves silence and insists on it.

Similarly, she does not tarry over emotions, as out of tune with the Gospel as idle discourses. The Lord has put us on our guard against these semi-scandalous utterances, welling up from our emotions, in which we merely "pity" the poor, instead of doing something to help them. The words of St. James the Apostle are stingingly apt: You visit your brothers in need, you give them a word of comfort and then leave them to their fate. In some ways, this is worse than just "passing by on the other side" like the priest and Levite on the road to Jericho: they at least did not seek a cut-price righteousness or an unmerited reputation for goodness. As against all the lies and hypocrisies of the world, how good and satisfying it is to watch Jeanne Jugan, active yet silent, going from bed to bed, only speaking when she has to or when charity requires, patiently "listening" to the woes confided to her, or hurrying along a street or a country road, while the rosary beads slip quietly between her fingers under her big black cape. That is what true charity is: this does not deceive, nor does it run the risk of being deceived.

"One day, perhaps, you will be sent out collecting. You won't like it. I have done it too; I didn't like it. I did it for God, for the poor."[1]

"Little one, if you want to be a good Little Sister, you must love God and the poor all you can, and forget about yourself."[2]

---

[1] Reported by Sr. Anatolie du Saint-Sacrement.

[2] Reported by Sr. Clémentine du Saint-Rosaire (Marie-Catherine Debard).

"Refuse God nothing."[3]

"This is madness!" exclaimed the wife of a highly placed official in Rennes,[4] on seeing Jeanne's plans and totting up her resources. Madness, yes, the madness of a free heart, where none of God's strength goes to waste, where generosity is not dispersed in idle talk, where every action proceeds from energy accumulated in the silence of prayer, where charity's undertakings know no limit imposed by considerations of self, where nothing is expended in vain.

The realism of this silent love, praying and at the same time shouldering prodigious undertakings, of this "good heart" in the Gospel sense of the term, by no means ruled by passion or emotion, is a stern rebuke to our more or less complicit lies.

This is what is meant by being like Jesus Christ.

[3] Reported by Sr. Séraphine du Saint-Esprit.

[4] Cf. Mme. de la Corbinière, *op. cit.*, p. 203. The Lady in question was almost certainly the wife of M. Alexandre Chevremont, Secretary General of the Sub-Prefecture of Ille-et-Vilaine until 1848. He later became sub-prefect of Saint-Malo and, after various other positions, mayor of Saint-Servan in 1875. Alexandre Chevremont published *Stances dediées à Jeanne Jugan*, Rennes 1846.

THE
FRUITS OF POVERTY

FAITH

By pulling at the golden thread of poverty, we have reached and brought to light Jeanne Jugan's hidden depths. One by one, her moral and religious qualities have appeared before our admiring gaze. Some of these however appear in higher relief than others, as focus for a wider or brighter radiance. And these focal points are what we are now going to study, the better to understand Jeanne Jugan's soul and the better to profit from her example.

Faith is the first of these to come to mind. And indeed, we have already given some thought to this. Our consideration of the deeper implications of poverty has shown us that at the very heart of poverty lies faith. Faith indeed is its key. Faith is what gives it efficacity and value. And since poverty played such a cardinal role in Jeanne's life, it is worth lingering over faith a little more.

We are all aware of the wealth contained in the word faith as used in Scripture by our Lord and by St. Paul. Pregnant with the most astounding promises, capable of every kind of miracle, how far removed this full-blooded and inestimable quality is from the wan notions which theological analysts extract, justifiably enough, for their purposes! The "Word of God" to which our faith responds is something quite different from a mere verbal pronouncement, to which as to any other we react, first by evaluating, then by assenting. The "Word of God," as well we know, is ultimately the "Word of God made flesh," the "Son of God," Jesus Christ. Every word issuing from his mouth, every act performed by him, and most of all that supreme act of his voluntary death on the cross, is inseparable from him. All his words are rich in his light and in his love; and in them, they bear life for those who receive them. His acts, which in their way are also words, are equally full of life, which he wants to communicate to us. Hence, the act of faith, in its fullest scriptural sense, involves and requires the same fullness on our part. Our response has to be commensurate with the Word. And hence, it draws our whole being into the encounter with him who has given us his whole being.

You may think this a very exalted plane from which to start talking about Jeanne Jugan's faith. But unless we start from here, we run the risk either of stopping short at the surface of her soul, or of depriving ourselves, by use of the word "faith" in its narrow, academic sense, of an enquiry which can lead us right into the recesses of her exemplary life.

St. Augustine, who well understood the riches of

faith, and who constantly kept his thought and
words at a level where faith retains its density of
meaning and spiritual value, provided theology
with several useful tools, which we are going to
use. Latin lends itself better than English, perhaps,
to the distinctions and alliterations of the saint and
we shall have to forgo these in translation. We can,
however, exploit the gist in the soundings which
we propose to make. And in English it is perfectly
acceptable to say that one believes someone (i.e.
what that person says); that one believes something; and, thirdly, that one believes in someone.
As regards Christ, faith entirely absorbs these three
meanings, including all these expressions in making
up the whole.

Let us consider Jeanne Jugan's living faith
through these three windows afforded to us by language, not losing sight, from whatever viewpoint,
of the fact that poverty is always there.

First of all, then, faith means: giving assent.

Christ speaks. He speaks to us about his Father.
He speaks to us about ourselves and our own destiny. He speaks to us about our duties. He inter-
prets our living present for us. He reveals what the
future holds in store for us. He explains the meaning of our sufferings to us, he calls them "crosses,"
since they are inseparable from his cross. He promises us happiness in his Kingdom. For us, he un-
masks the deceits and lies in our own hearts.

Faith consists, primarily, then in saying: Christ
is right, this is true; and in saying it without reser-
vation from the bottom of our heart. Even though

it may strike us as hard to believe: "Who can accept this?" said the Jews about the Bread of Life. Even if it seems beyond our strength: "In such conditions, it would be better not to get married," said the disciples when faced with the severity of the marriage law. Even if it seems "impossible to human beings," like being saved amid the riches of the world. Faith is "unconditional," or nil.

With all this said, and now plunging our gaze into Jeanne Jugan's soul, we discover the presence of this first form of faith. Better perhaps to call it an aspect, rather than a form, so that we are not later tempted to judge her faith as summary and elementary; so that we may, on the contrary, learn from her what our faith should be.

Jeanne Jugan is not the one to know how to distinguish between truth and truth and to know which one to believe and which one not to believe; and indeed, she absolutely and instinctively refuses to do anything of the sort. For her, what God says, what she reads in the Gospel, what the Church has taught her through her catechism: this is all true. "God speaks": this is enough for her. The area in which her faith is apparently most tested and where it appears in full perfection, is precisely that of poverty. She believes that the Father watches over us and will no more forsake his children than let the birds of the air go hungry. Her faith in the divine promises, contained in Revelation and concerned with the fatherhood of God, this she lives directly and heroically. She believes that "God will provide," from the moment that he summons her.

"Divine Providence was her repose, in joy as in sorrow:

'God is our Father, let us put our trust in him!' "[1]

"Yes indeed, it does seem mad, it does seem impossible, but if God is with us, it will be done."[2] And events proved her right, as against the arguments of human prudence. "It does seem mad," yes, if God is left out of account. But wise, if you take him into account and also count on him. And Jeanne Jugan was right. The truth of faith is an indivisible whole. Brains are not all alike, some seeing more, some seeing fewer, subtleties in doctrine, some producing more, and some fewer, problems; vocations are not all alike, requiring greater or less knowledge and grasp of fact ... but there is only one way of believing: Jeanne Jugan's way.

Believing means trusting someone's word. And this entails also believing something. What is Jeanne Jugan's creed?

There are all sorts of answers to this, and some of them very good ones. One of them certainly is that her creed was that of her baptism and catechism. But this is not saying enough. We should hardly be doing her justice if we were to envisage her as applying her faith to a concatenation of truths, set out for her one after the other. Things were simpler for her than that. This whole gamut

---

[1] Reported by Sr. Catherine de tous les saints (Marie-Ludivine Emprin).

[2] Mme. de la Corbinière, *op. cit.*, p. 203.

of things to be believed and of things to be loved, can be summed up in one simple truth. Jesus was her reason for believing. He was also truly the object of her faith. In him converge all individual truths, not one of which would she have been willing to sacrifice. For, not one of them, for her, was separable from Jesus. In him, she saw the Father. In him, she saw herself. In him, she saw her fellow-man.

And of this, what better sign or proof can we find than the way in which she habitually regarded her old people, the poor whom Jesus had confided to her, and of whom He said that she must find him in them? "This is Jesus," she tells the young novices, with that marvellous simplicity of faith, as though her very soul were exploding with joy, in awareness of the gift given to her and of what that would entail in self-giving for her. "It's Jesus." All Jeanne's faith is concentrated in this single point. For her, there is nothing beyond this unique object, where all truths, all duties, all promises are one.

"We have him in all our houses. Go and find him when your patience and strength give out and you feel alone and helpless. Jesus is waiting for you in the chapel. Say to him: 'You know, dear Jesus, what is going on . . . You are all I have . . . Come and help me.' And then go . . . and don't worry about how you are going to manage. That you have told God about it is enough. He has a good memory."[3]

[3] Reported by Sr. Marie de Saint-Romain.

"When you get old, you won't be able to see All I can see now is God."[4]

Here again, what a lesson! How much we need to keep dipping our sense of faith in springs like these! What a gulf lies between this soul grown single-minded in the truth, and our own poor distracted spirits, suffering in our distraction, losing our way in our creed as though in a virgin forest, and all because we do not have sufficient faith to manage to, or to consent, to fix our gaze on what is the centre and the whole!

What Jeanne Jugan believed is what we have to believe: not more, not less. Before the Creed developed to meet the needs of passing time, it consisted of these words, as history bears witness: "I believe in Jesus Christ." Whoever says this with all his heart and all his mind and all his soul, has said all that there is to be said.

But we are well aware that believing in Jesus Christ is something quite different from merely believing someone, some credible witness, or from believing something, even about Jesus. Believing in Jesus Christ means more than giving assent to the truth about someone. Believing in Jesus Christ means giving ourselves with all our soul, in trust, in humility, in love, in adoration and in service, to him whom we acknowledge as Lord and who, by asking for our faith, gives himself as completely to us. Jesus has not made some revelation to us; he has told us everything as between friends. He has not given us

---

[4] Reported by Sr. Céline de l'Ascension.

a little light or a little strength; he has offered us communion with him, unity with him and with his Father. He is our God become our brother. And by virtue of this, he demands our unconditional loyalty. By virtue of this, he himself is all truth.

I believe in Jesus Christ: this is the fundamental statement of our faith, the unique formula in which all is said and whence all else proceeds, the formula in which our whole being expends itself in assent and in self-giving.

Such was the faith that permeated Jeanne Jugan's every action, every step, every word. Idle to isolate traces of it here or there. It is not more detectable in her contemplation of the crucifix held tight to her heart, than in the Hail Mary said in the wind and rain. No more, but no less. And no less in the thank you said to a benefactor than in the good morning said to an old woman. No less, but no more. No more in the humanly-speaking crazy courage of making a new foundation, than in the silent isolation of her cell. Faith is not here, not there. It is everywhere, when faith is truly faith. Faith cannot be reduced to isolated actions; it is not an abstraction; it takes, cannot but take, the entire soul; it goes to him to whom alone the soul can give herself: the Father who is in Heaven and who makes himself known in his Son.

But we have not said everything about faith until we have reminded ourselves that it also means trusting someone. Of itself, it stretches out towards something else. Its inherent nature is a waiting for something more complete. Faith in what is said, in anticipation of that direct revelation of the truth in which faith vanishes.

I believe in Jesus Christ: this means: "I await the ineffable joy of meeting in the light of Heaven."

And on Jeanne Jugan's dying lips, we find this final act of faith, already, it would seem, the beginning of that light: "Eternal Father, open your gates today to the most wretched of your little daughters, to one though who most earnestly longs to see you."[5]

What a sublime thing faith is when it is truly lived!

We can hardly tell where faith ends and where love begins. The last words of the "Centurion" Psichari, at the end of the "journey" which brought him back to his God, rise instinctively to our lips after watching Jeanne Jugan live out her faith: "My God, how easy it is to love you, after all!"

[5] Mme. de la Corbinière, *op. cit.*, p. 348.

ABANDONMENT

Faith and charity, by virtue of their object, are both by way of being absolutes. You cannot believe in God by halves; he can only ask us for, and we can only give Him, an unconditional loyalty, since he is Truth, and any doubts about the reliability of his word would be tantamount to blasphemy. Similarly, the first commandment, echoed by so much of Christ's teaching, insists that our attitude towards God be to love him with all our being, to be willing to sacrifice everything for him, since he is our unique and absolute Good, and any limit set to our love or to our obedience would constitute the fault of all faults: and true death of the soul.

We have already seen how Jeanne Jugan lived out the demands of faith and charity under the specific form of poverty. The word abandonment is traditionally applied to this radical attitude, in which God alone can be the object: an attitude exemplified in high degree by the saints. God shines through their lives; all their actions are performed specifically for him; and hence, their lives are marked by this abandonment, and their actions, despite hesitations and fresh starts, express this abandonment at every moment of their lives. And hence, the saints are an indispensable model for Christians, whose vocation is in no way basically different from theirs, and whose faith and charity are not different from theirs in nature, if unfortunately in degree.

Christ's abandonment was not the abandonment of faith, but of full comprehension and absolute love for his Father; and this too must be the supreme law of our own abandonment: we must "live for him" as "he lives for us." We know what this means: the need for obedience, that true expression of our love for God: "Who keeps my commandments, that is the one who loves Me"... "The world must know that I always do God's will." We know, and the Gospel tells us, what this means: the inward "handing-over" of ourselves "to the end," not stopping at the gift of life, not stopping at honour, to the last drop of our blood.

Abandonment, this "letting-go," the complete giving over of ourselves, "mind, body, life" as St. Paul says to his Corinthians, sets the very seal of authenticity on the life of Jeanne Jugan. Let us consider the matter more closely.

Primarily, abandonment looks towards God. It is a supreme act of love, and only secondarily detachment from some or other human possession. Even so, this secondary aspect — the outward, observable one — is what appears the more striking.

Abandonment means first denying oneself. To abandon yourself, you must start by abandoning things. You see, God's call is addressed to us, not to the artificial riches fettering and weighing us down. We can only "fall into God," once we have consented to cast off these anchors. Not only in intention, but always, to some degree at least, in fact. The day will of course come when death does the job for us: "We brought nothing with us into the world when we came, and it is very sure that we shall take nothing out with us when we leave," says St. Paul.[1] But a break like this has to be prepared for, and we know how Jesus helped his disciples to prepare for it. They were to "leave all," in order to follow him. Now, there are few examples of a more radical, or of a more willingly accepted, abandonment than that demanded of Jeanne Jugan: the abandonment of material things, the progressive impoverishment, are as nothing in her life when compared with the threefold and absolute way in which she was "dispossessed" of her work; it was taken out of her hands without more ado. And people only bothered to remember her afterward when they needed her to get them out of a mess. They contrived, by a kind of miracle, to erect a wall of silence round her to which she lent herself, out of what she supposed to be obedience and from the moment that the work looked like being a success. Even so, she was perfectly aware that she was being underrated, and perfectly aware of the worth of what other people chose to call

[1] *I Timothy 6:7.*

"their rights." The essential work had been done,
the instruments were all to hand, she did not count
any more: and hence, she obeyed; in future she
would obey instead of giving the orders; she would
respect the improvised superior whom she herself
had trained and, in all humility, believe that the
latter was capable of doing the job. And, as regards
herself, she would even be forgotten at the Coun-
cil, which she was supposed to attend; she was
aware of this, but if she said so, she said so without
a trace of bitterness.

As for the man responsible for this strange state
of affairs, eventually the Holy See, when better
informed, was to realize what had been going on.
Once summoned to Rome, M. Le Pailleur never
went back to Brittany and never recovered the
office of Superior, bestowed on himself in the first
place by himself. And so at long last, the truth
came to light. But what interests us here is not the
case of this unfortunate psychopath, but the state
of soul of the woman who endured the effects of
his actions and arbitrary decisions. . . . He had
helped the small informal group to develop into a
regular community. He had done so with the per-
mission of his bishop. . . . No one had realized that
an inherent psychological weakness was already
impelling him, and would impel him more and
more, to imagine himself the founder, and hence to
push the willingly defenceless foundress into the
most absolute shade. Jeanne Jugan, being completely realistic, was well aware that the ship was
well and truly launched; the choice of a superior to
replace her, the Sisters' election notwithstanding,

did not strike her as contrary to the interests of the community and of the aged poor whom it was meant to serve. Offering no resistance, not upsetting the development of the newborn project by causing domestic conflict, back into the ranks she stepped.

Renunciation of this sort, without fuss or protest, when faced with an eclipse soon to be total and to last for a quarter of a century, is truly astounding. Indeed, we have to say heroic. It is hard to imagine an equilibrium of soul capable of sustaining inner peace and serenity unaffected by such shocks. What truly superhuman strength, what incredible resilience of character!

Or to put it more precisely: what immense love!

Abandonment must not be seen from the angle of what is sacrificed, but of whom that sacrifice is made to.

"No one can take my life away from me, I choose to give it up," says the Lord. No renunciation has any value unless it flows from a personal act of will. The passive attractions of renunciation are illusory. True renunciation has to be active. The headsman does not triumph over the martyr. As the old Office hymn says, the true conquerors are not the wretched executioners but the martyr who voluntarily dies under their blows. Only, the love which impels us to such sacrifices, is alien to all ostentation, leaving murderous brutality the illusion of success: the true acts of a martyr are overwhelmingly discreet; the exchange with his judges is supremely, eloquently reticent: "Are you a

Christian?" — "I am." The rest is literature, and the flashing exchanges between victim and executioner in later stories are tedious rather than edifying.

Reference here to documents of the past is not misplaced. Not only because the sacrifice taking place is of the same heroic order: Jeanne Jugan offers her heart's blood; but because the true victor in these conflicts is the same: Jesus Christ. True, the battle makes love grow all the stronger, but the battle is itself both the work and sign of love. Love for Christ is its origin and its end, as it was in the action of the sinful woman at Simon's dinner party:[2] the Word of the Lord bears a double construction, each equally true: love is at once cause and effect.

Jeanne Jugan displays a heart so utterly filled with love for Christ that not even the rudest blows can shake it. "In our worries, in our troubles, in the way other people look down on us, we must always say: Blessed be God! Thank you, my God! or, Glory be to God!"[3] "We have been grafted on to the Cross."[4] There is no hint of anyone's having noticed any sign of dismay in her behaviour when she was elbowed aside; I do not mean merely of protest, but of any deeper, inner struggle. Nothing said, of course; words were not for her when they were not necessary, still less when inopportune. Not only no words, but not even a trace of behav-

---

[2] *Luke* 7.

[3] Mme. de la Corbinière, *op. cit.*, p. 32.

[4] Reported by Sr. Scholastique (Jeanne Tassel).

iour which could have been construed as reflecting an inner conflict. Jeanne Jugan stepped down and disappeared, just as she had stepped on to the stage in the first place, in simple and discreet obedience to what she thought to be the will of God and the wish of Jesus. And we may suppose that even this incredible sacrifice, this virtual annihilation, notwithstanding the effort it demanded of her, was assented to with the same humility as the lowliest of her day-to-day tasks: because God wished it, for love of him, and for the good of his poor. Jeanne Jugan regarded herself as an instrument in God's hands for serving them. She loved Jesus, his will and his poor, too much to fight back or to oppose. What would have happened if, instead of silently renouncing, she had energetically reacted to assert her rights, or merely to help the Little Sisters round her to realize the enormity of this unjustifiable and arbitrary act of authority? Perhaps the work would have gone on? It is by no means sure, for in the initial stages all projects are fragile. But the Institute would certainly always have borne the scar, if nothing worse, of this first conflict: a conflict which, whether justifiable or not, would certainly have been based on considerations of human rights and wrongs; as a result of which, the Little Sisters would never have become quite what they are now. The love that silenced Jeanne Jugan's mouth, has probably made a greater contribution than any other, to the birth of a type of soul enriching the Church forever.

There are other forms of abandonment. But hers unmistakably corresponds to that of the lamb who,

in Isaiah's words, is dumb before his shearer. Jesus
fulfilled Isaiah's prophecy. He let himself be put to
death without a word.

And it is Jeanne Jugan's glory and the exceptional value of her example, that she so faithfully
reproduced the characteristics of her Lord. In her
was that same Spirit to guide and sustain her.

JOY

In the promises and prayers of the Holy Books, joy is ever associated with peace.

Joy, joy peaceful, deep and unperturbed, radiates from Jeanne Jugan's life. Even the dramatic and far-reaching events which we have been considering could not deprive her of this grace or quench its radiance.

"At the eleventh station, when she was doing the Way of the Cross, we used to hear her say that she was fixed to the Cross with her Saviour, and that she hoped to carry it joyfully till she died."[1]

She was happy, she wanted the Little Sisters to be happy too.

This joy is the product of the presence and the love of Jesus, which no human attachment can limit or spoil. At the same time, Jeanne also regarded joy as a duty. Joy is one of the Little Sisters' vocational obligations. They are to sow joy around them. Their job is to exorcize sorrow, that ever-recurring complaint of the aged. Jeanne knew that

[1] Reported by Sr. Céline de l'Ascension.

the condition of the aged disposes them to sorrow, that they are afraid of it, that it comes back again and again as the bitter fruit of loneliness and helplessness. Literally then, Little Sisters did not have the right to be sad; and this was what Jeanne was forever telling the novices at the Tour Saint-Joseph. She wanted to see them cheerful, with radiant, happy faces, shedding light on the aged for whom the shadows were slowly drawing in.

"I am not telling you that the aged won't make you suffer, but do not let it show. Be generous-hearted!"[2]

"Little ones, you must always be cheerful. Our old folk do not like long faces."[3]

What kind of joy is this? For a start, it is worlds away from what people commonly mean by joy. It is not assuming a mask to keep up the spirits or to defy fate. Nor is it that emotional excitement better described as pleasure. Jeanne Jugan's joy and that of her Sisters comes entirely from within. It is not something sought, it is something given from above as something extra. It is the sign of a perfect harmony existing between their lives and the people and things with whom and which they have to do.

Musical harmony by which, first dawning on the ear, a sense of satisfaction pervades the whole being, provides the best analogy for the birth and abiding presence of this kind of joy. The events of

---

[2] Reported by Sr. Honorine de la Trinité (Marie-Anne Jouan).

[3] Reported by Sr. Noël-Joséphine.

life, as they impinge, can make this sense of joy
apparent to those who are no more than bystanders, while in the souls of those in whom the harmony resounds, each time a newer and more vivid
awareness is brought to birth.

Joy severe and deep found, yet rich and sweet —
we hear it speaking through Jeanne Jugan's lips:
she is happy in owning nothing and in owing all to
God. This is a very different thing from a morbid
state of self-inflicted suffering, or the proud satisfaction of stoical self-conquest. If Jeanne Jugan
gives her joy full voice, she does not do so primarily because she has nothing, but because, having nothing, she has confidently been able to put
herself in God's hands and thus experienced the
joy promised to those who are led by the Holy
Spirit. She is free — to love Christ and to cleave to
him.

And this joy is also the joy which comes from
prayer. Jeanne Jugan must have experienced
(indeed, we can say, undoubtedly experienced —
when we think of the experiences of the saints)
those moments which the mystics call "dark
nights." Day by day, the Lord gave her the joy
which is born of love. Events which might appear
inimical to it, did not disturb it. Instead, they only
revealed the extent of its riches. Far from destroy-
ing joy, the difficulties nourished and reinforced it.
The image of Jeanne tightly clutching her crucifix
under her cloak, of Jeanne on her knees for hours
before the Blessed Sacrament in the chapel, are not
images of a tormented personality, but of someone
whose joyful serenity remained untroubled, be the

task and position assigned to her by the Lord what
they might.

Her joy, then, is one of deep assent, confirmed
by experience and rewarded by God's grace. When
God's will is apparently to reduce her to silence
and to treat her as of apparently little worth, or
when contrariwise it urges her forward to actions
and undertakings apparently beyond her means,
she, as an obedient and supple instrument in God's
hand, goes forward in the tranquil assurance of
absolute trust in God, rejoicing to feel herself perfectly available to him.

St. Thomas teaches that joy is the fruit of love.
He is right. And this exactly sums up all that can
be said about the joy radiating from Jeanne's life.
But love, clearly, must be understood in its proper
sense. What St. Thomas means is charity, the divine
gift bringing us into communion with God's will
and requiring nothing for itself in return. We can
say more: the joy born of communion with God
expands to the fullest extent in Jeanne Jugan,
being the fruit of a generously expansive love. Joy
in her soul is total, because the gift of herself is
made without reserve. In her, love for God is not
merely the ground for dialogue with God, but the
principle of service and devotion to other people.
As God finds his own joy in pouring out himself,
so Jeanne finds hers in a tranquil and tirelessly
repeated self-giving. The aged owe their joy to her,
but give it back to her: she finds this joy in the
very love which she expends in serving them, and
this love is none other than the very love of God
passing through them to her.

Impossible to imagine the joy of Jeanne Jugan and her Little Sisters as existing independently of the joy which they give to the aged in their charge. The joy on the Little Sisters' faces reflects the joy aroused on the careworn faces of the poor, just as the joy of the aged reflects the inner joy of souls tending them in devotion to the Lord.

We cannot compartmentalize Jeanne's life, putting her relationship with God on one side, and her relationship with the aged for whom she has assumed responsibility on the other. She finds God and finds her own self in giving herself to him. The total deprivation to which, without outward or even inward form, she has given assent, makes it possible for grace to work in her unimpeded. And within her, therefore, she bears all the fruits of grace, not least a kind of joyous lustre — like a splendidly ripe fruit, delicious to the taste, but even before that, miraculously satisfying to the eye.

"Come, little ones, let us sing the glory of our Risen Jesus," said Jeanne Jugan to the novices, one Easter morning.[4] "Do you know who made this?" she asked a Little Sister, pointing to a small wild flower. "God did!" and in grateful tones, she added: "He is our Bridegroom!"[5]

Jeanne Jugan condemns and banishes sadness. She regards it as a kind of fraud practised on the aged. They have a right to joy as to everything else, and even more to joy than to anything else. Since

[4] Reported by Sr. Aimée de Saint-Francois (Joséphine Lemoine).

[5] Reported by Sr. Angélique de Saint-Paul (Adèle Prével).

they so badly need it. The joy of Little Sisters is an essential sign of God's love encountering theirs. A Little Sister turned in on herself and on her sorrows, deprives others of a treasure given to her in trust for them. People gladly take joy in what they own. But the truest joy resides in not owning. For thus we become an instrument for God, who passes through us, filling us with him. "There is more joy in giving than in receiving": — a saying of the Lord recorded by St. Paul, whose whole life bears it out. How often he wished his converts joy, how often bade them for their part rejoice, how often gave voice to his own joy! But always by self-giving and willing sacrifice.

Here again, at the wellsprings, we see poverty, true poverty. The true poor are joyful because they converse with God alone.

LITTLENESS

In studying the soul of Jeanne Jugan and her Sisters, we cannot but be struck by two distinct impressions. On the one hand, we see such a store of moral vigour, of patience and of energy. And on the other, we note a fundamental aspiration to join the underprivileged, in Christ — an aspiration very closely attuned to Gospel precept. The world at large has hence been right in awarding Jeanne Jugan's daughters the title of "Little" Sisters of the Poor. And Jeanne Jugan herself ratified this general judgment: she it was who more or less introduced the word "littleness" into spiritual literature. For her daughters, "littleness" is law. "Be very little," she constantly urged the novices.

"Above all, learn to be truly humble. Once you are in a house, stay very little. If you keep the spirit of humility, of simplicity, of littleness as of a little family, never seeking the esteem of the influential, you will give cause for other people to bless God and you will obtain the conversion of souls. But, were you to become big and proud, the Congregation would fall."[1]

"Be grateful for your vocation. Let yourselves be formed by the spirit of littleness."[2]

We are talking, of course, about humility, the humility of the truly poor, poor in that they have nothing, and poor in that they want nothing. Destitution like this puts you at the bottom of the scale of values as held by a world where possessions are the real criterion of respect. For poor people of this sort, however, all forms of human greatness seem incompatible with their destiny. They take, as though by right, the lowest place. This needs our closer study, since there is scope for error here. The world, with its altogether different conception of life, tends automatically to misjudge and deprecate a taste for littleness. The world does not understand, is embarrassed by it. At best, for the world it remains a mystery — and one preferably ignored.

Now, plainly a Christian would to some degree be denying his Master, were he to try to ignore what is so intentionally marked a feature of Christ.

Some people may perhaps feel a little uncomfortable, at the sight of this adjective stuck on to the name of the Sisters. Isn't there something rather sloppy and sentimental about it? But then, you have only to see how St. Thérèse of the Child

[1] Reported by Sr. Hortense de Sainte-Anne (Marie-Mélanie Bernard).

[2] Reported by Sr. Marie de Saint-Bernardin (Marie-Anne Coquaud).

Jesus used the word, to realize that there need not be anything childish there. It exactly expresses a state of soul by which men and women are made capable of daily heroism. The greatest of the saints, of the undisputed saints, St. Francis of Assisi for instance, have all used it. And this invests the word with dignity. The diminutive form "poverello" in Italian does not diminish the stature of the Poor Man of Assisi.

This littleness resides deep in the soul, not in any childishness of word or deed. Naturally, ostentatious actions have no place here, nor verbiage that inflates and falsifies emotions and will, to issue in hot air. The littleness of someone like Jeanne Jugan is the very negation of worldly greatness. There is no question of impressing other people or of exalting herself. There is no question of shining. Littleness completely excludes any such ambitions and illusions. As far as the world is concerned, the Little Sister may disappear entirely, as Jeanne Jugan did; and, be her activities or her responsibilities what they may, her heart and deepest dispositions remain unchanged. Never has the Gospel promise been taken more literally: if any type of greatness be wished or desired, it is precisely that conferred by self-effacement.

"We must learn humbly to efface ourselves in everything that God requires us to do, as though mere instruments for his work."[3]

But this disinterest is in itself only meaningful when related to some higher, governing entity,

---

[3] Reported by Sr. Joséphine Albert (Marie-Joseph Camoz).

central to all and round which all activity revolves.
The littleness of a Jeanne Jugan is an affirmation
of life conceived in other terms from those in
which the world conceives it: a willing abandonment into the hands of him who governs all for the
good of the world, for the good of others and for
one's own good too.

"Yes, indeed, God has been very good to me. He
has done all this, I am only his humble servant."[4]

And hence, this personal littleness not only does
not militate against great enterprises and bold plans
but actually becomes the instrument for inconceiv-
ably vast constructions. Works are born to hands
refusing any human honours but owing all to God.
Jeanne undertakes nothing on the spur of the
moment or on her personal initiative. She waits for
a sign from God, for the right moment to come.
An intuition coming from on high, makes her
aware that God is reserving her for some great purpose. She does not try to anticipate, either by
thought or deed, what this may be. Years go by,
the intuition all the while sufficing to prevent her
from straying from the road where she will eventually encounter the Lord and his command. Now
comes the sign from God, and forthwith all her
reserves of strength go into action. The work grows
and grows under this humble woman's hand: the
bedroom turns into a dormitory; the dormitory
turns into a house; the house burgeons out into
new buildings; foundation follows foundation.
Everything that she touches grows, like the grains

---

[4] Reported by Sr. Catherine de tous les saints.

of wheat or loaves of bread miraculously multi-
plied by the Lord.

Only when compared with human greatness, does
the quality of spiritual littleness appear. And a very
positive quality it is. Indeed, true greatness must be
measured by it — greatness that belongs to the
order of charity, if we may echo Paschal. "He who
makes himself little like a child, is the one who will
be great in the Kingdom of Heaven." The word of
the Lord means just what it says — it is not a figure
of speech. And indeed, "true" greatness, as the
Gospel says, is the greatness that resists time, the
greatness that reveals itself by faith, the greatness
that is measured by love. This greatness alone
abides, to lead into the world of the divine, which
is the world of the eternal. It is no paradox for us
to say that the firmer this littleness becomes, the
greater grows the soul.

Littleness puts us into true relationship with
God. It leads into all truth. It disposes us to receive
whatever is given. It is not primarily a renouncing
of something, but a capacity for acquiring something else of supreme worth. Nothing is higher than
humility, say St. Ambrose, since humility is highest
placed of all. Once again, as when we were talking
about poverty and sacrifice, we find a similar
ambiguity. Littleness ensures the elimination of
what human judgment and language alike assume
to be worth having, to be the only thing worth
having. Hence, we tend to think of a loss or a
diminution. But in fact, by virtue of this apparent
loss, the soul aligns herself precisely on God, she

mounts towards him, she lightens herself to rise, she participates in God's own greatness, besides which human greatness is as nothing.

Our Lord gave littleness its distinctive name: he revealed the secret of it when talking about "childhood." In making herself little, under the impact of grace, the soul works her own "rebirth." And she consents, as to God, to becoming "heir" to all his good things. The soul does not regard this as greatness in the human sense of the word; this would, of course, be a contradiction. Nonetheless, greatness it is. The soul is aware of growing greater, but only in the sense that she feels the love of God growing within her; and thus, she "dilates," if we may use the word, though human eyes cannot observe the change.

So we do have to enter this light and rise to this level before we can understand Jeanne Jugan's littleness. It is just the same as that of St. Thérèse of the Child Jesus. Jeanne Jugan does not use our units of measure; or rather we might say, that she dwells in a world where greatness as the world sees it has no more meaning. She does not despise the world: she loves God. She does not seek to be little in the eyes of men. She puts herself into the best possible relationship with God, and this allows her to love more entirely: and thus she finds herself going backwards along the road instinctively followed by the rest of mankind.

That this is not a negative way, immediately appears from her relationship with other human beings. The love of God untrammelled can deploy itself unopposed. Having no considerations left where self is concerned, Jeanne Jugan's soul becomes capable of loving others as God loves, and indeed with God's own love. As though by nature, she turns with God to procure the good of other creatures. At St. Paul says, in her eyes they become more important than herself. She serves them as her superiors. She is free to love them. Instinctively, she gives herself entirely to them. And the instinct is that of God's grace dwelling within her. Men call this service. In it, they see a degree of humiliation. But this is in fact true greatness, the greatness of love, the greatness of God. For what the Gospel calls brotherly love, making no distinction and going out to all, to the furthest extent of self-giving in imitation of the Lord, is not a work of ours. And hence it is often called by a name not properly its; or people are content to sense a mystery here, without penetrating further. For littleness is really another name for the love of God, a divine gift making recipient and user great.

" 'Jeanne, what are we to call you now?' — 'The humble servant of the poor!' "[5] In renouncing all greatness, Jeanne Jugan is only following her Master. That is all she wants to do. All she does is to respond to the Father's will. And thus she encounters the very greatness of God.

---

[5] Canon Helleu, *op. cit.*, p. 80.

LUCIDITY

What are we to call the quality that made Jeanne Jugan's activities so remarkable and that made her such a remarkable woman too? — The adventurous wisdom guiding the Little Sisters through the years must be attributable to her; hers were the successive early foundations, the first implantings of the earliest seeds. The traditional name for this quality, or rather for this virtue, is prudence but, fine as it is, the word has developed overtones as misleading as they are unpleasing, some of them suggesting an element of calculation, others of caution rather than of initiative. For want of a better one, let us call it "lucidity."

A shadow seems to hover over the early years of her creative life. And we might be tempted to blame Jeanne Jugan for the tiresome, and in some respects evil, presence and actions of M. Le Pailleur.

First, however, be it said that the beginnings of any great work of God have almost always involved, whether obviously or obscurely, the presence of someone fated to hinder the designs of Providence: whether by opposing them and trying to prevent them from developing, or by trying to seize control of them and divert them to greater or lesser degree from their true course. Sometimes this is done openly and in absolute good faith, sometimes not so openly, and again sometimes quite unscrupulously.

Jeanne Jugan had already been dead for seven years when the ecclesiastical authorities began to entertain their first doubts about M. Le Pailleur's probity of action. And, once irrefutable proof had been obtained, the authorities took another three years to make up their minds before taking the necessary measures. Up to this point, M. Le Pailleur had been regarded as a saint, as a miracle-worker, as a true mystic.

It would appear now that M. Le Pailleur had never been able to reconcile himself to the presence of this woman, as upright as she was unselfish, simply and steadfastly committed, animated by a charity as pure as it was ostentatious. And it would also appear that Jeanne Jugan, without saying so or letting it show, did not feel at ease in close proximity with him. Without judging him, without going against general opinion, she allowed herself to be set aside, to God confiding the future of a work which she knew to be of God, and which she wished God himself to direct. We must honour her for this and, rather than regard it as a lack of prudence, see it as a perfect example of wisdom and humility.

Given what she herself was in a position to know

and what other people were in a position to see, all she could do was to leave the rest to Providence. Her own destiny kept her at a distance, and other people made it their business to see that she stayed there. And that was that.

Lucidity, permeated through and through with humility and charity, is never wanting in Jeanne Jugan.

Her prudence, in the proper, noble sense of the word, is the highest form of Christian prudence. Characteristic of this prudence and often very disconcerting to human eyes, is the primacy of those means and resources which Péguy used to call "poor means." This kind of prudence is never so assured, never so blessed in its decisions, never so fruitful in its results, never so persevering, as when aware of being destitute, apparently at least, of everything that sustains and nourishes human action. The fewer resources there are, the more can be done, and the more is done. And why? Because the less the support given by the world, the more support has to be sought from God, and the more God's own wisdom and strength can be used.

What armed Jeanne Jugan above all for her activities was her simple, unconditional trust in Christ, whom she felt to be present within her, and whom she asked for whatever she needed; whom she saw present in the aged, and who made her capable of miracles in serving them. The lever to move mountains that rose across her path was her faith, her love. Christian prudence is first and foremost a fruitful and active reliance on God the ordainer of

all things. Jeanne Jugan, tireless in prayer as in
humble self-effacement, is a wonderful and heroic
example of this. And it is hardly surprising that
such activity as hers should have been so instantly
and generously crowned with success. Her activity
was that of God within her: her wisdom, God's
wisdom. The true miracle occurred within. The few
small facts that we have mentioned in connection
with the collecting round derive from that same
prudential inspiration as, for example, the replies
of Joan of Arc, harassed by keen-witted judges:
"Do not worry about what to do, or about what to
say: the Holy Spirit within you will be there to
answer for you." Jeanne Jugan had much experience of that.

But the presence and intervention of the Holy
Spirit, prompt, easy, perfect, divine as they are, are
never intended to dispense human beings from the
normal round of activity, nor from mobilizing all
available resources in God's service.

This is why Jeanne Jugan appears to us, not as a
mystic in the pejorative sense of the word, but as a
courageously active, intelligent and sagaciously
enterprising woman. Her works speak for her. She
knows what she wants. She knows what help to ask
for. Admittedly, she is trying to do the impossible,
but this is because God assures her that this is what
can be done; nor does she expect to be granted an
instant and effortless result. She prays, she sees,
she seeks the means, she persists, she achieves. Her
house is as orderly as her thought: she goes to her
goal with resolute, patient wisdom. When the bread

runs out, she does not wait for more to fall from
heaven; she sets out to look for some. What she can
no longer do in the restricted space of her bedroom, she seeks and finds the means to do somewhere else in a larger house. When this is not large
enough, she starts to build. For her, "order" is
indeed a virtue. In her eyes, it is the sign not only
of a well-run house and of old people truly loved,
but above all of a mind well controlled, clear-
sighted, planning and putting into effect, trusting
in grace at each stage to bring it to a good end.

Bergson, who so admired the active, realistic
robustness of St. Teresa of Avila and St. Joan of
Arc, would just as much have admired this other
fruit of grace, this humble, resolute, tenacious
woman, whose hands were so prolific in good
works.

Jeanne Jugan's "instructions" to her collecting
sisters and her advice to her novices are little mas-
terpieces of wisdom and Christian prudence. The
task undertaken is a hard one, as she knows, and
the Virgin Mary whose example and help she
invokes is truly "Mother of Wisdom" for her.
Rereading the advice given by Jeanne Jugan to her
collecting sisters is like finding ourselves at a point
where many lights converge: a perfect harmony
between love for the poor; the desire to provide
them with what they need; the acceptance of
humility to gain this end; an infinitely sensitive
respect for other people whose generosity is never
to be forced; absolute confidence that grace will let
the means be found; ceaseless prayer; the rigorous
programme of work; choice of places, of people, of

collecting routes. Nothing is left to chance or to improvisation. God only helps those who help themselves: such is the implicit rule of this charitable activity. It is all so simple, so modest, so direct, that we are barely aware of all the thought, work, human and material considerations that have gone into it. This is the truly Christian virtue, so perfect indeed that we do not even notice it, like the perfectly functioning mechanism of a machine. Christian activity is a work of love. It sets all our resources to work in the service of this love. Christian activity goes to its goal, dissipating nothing of itself on the way to impress the casual observer. The miracle of "things being just so" down to the smallest detail is an honour offered exclusively to God.

EFFICACITY

By what criteria can we judge a life's achievement? What is not extinguished with life is known to God alone, to him alone what is to be garnered into Heaven. Even so, certain things are left for us to see; and on these we have no choice but to bring our human judgment to bear — on the remains, more or less beautiful, more or less extensive, more or less enduring.

Jeanne Jugan's work is beautiful: so many houses radiant with joy have sprung into being from her charity. Jeanne Jugan's work is vast: it extends over five continents. Each house is a microcosm of the world, with Little Sisters of every nationality working in it. Jeanne Jugan's work is enduring: it is still with us after buoyantly lasting for more than a century.

Her work does not seek, but need not fear, comparison with other contemporary works. For people with eyes to see, it has the dimensions of God's own charity, surpassing what man can either conceive or desire.

But here forthwith we must forestall any mis-
understanding.

Throughout these pages, in our attempt to
explore something of Jeanne Jugan's poverty, we
have, behind the work of the foundress, been
forced at every step to discern the great and true
Protagonist of this epic. By now, it must be
obvious to everyone that the work has primarily
been the work of God. Jeanne Jugan's strength
derives from what she is and remains in God's
hand: alone, she would have been nothing.

In the first hour of her existence, someone
knocked at her door. She heard the message dis-
tinctly, and she remembered its strong and simple
terms: a job was waiting for her, although she did
not know what. She therefore prepared for it.
Her preparation could not be specialized, since
she still did not know in the least what God
wanted, but was rather a preparation in depth,
since what was required was not knowledge of
some skill, but simple availability to the hands of
him who would one day use her for his purposes.
God disposed and made malleable the heart and
mind which he was going to need. He helped
them to acquire the essential qualities of abandonment, of prayer, of enterprising, wholehearted
obedience, which he would need.

And when the moment came, Jeanne had an
unburdened and unfettered heart to put at God's
disposal. She was free. God would be free to act
in her as he pleased. Nothing was less passive or
inert than the instrument thus fully prepared. Its
activity was directed in advance towards him who

meant to use it for his purpose.

Jeanne Jugan's efficacy is God's own efficacy.

The next point that has to be made is that the primary achievement over which we must linger is Jeanne Jugan herself.

The wonderful thing is not so much the spreading of her work throughout the world, as the pure and beautiful grandeur of a heart, selected by God to achieve this work. He bound it to himself from the beginning in the silence of humble loyalty. He took her up, took her up again and again, as though happy to play with a tool so utterly in his power. He detached her, one by one, from all the human props, which as far as we others are concerned are the normal methods of action, but which the power and love of God can replace: since means too can hold us back, whereas God desires a soul which is absolutely free for him.

Father, mother, family, friendships, material possessions: God asked her to sacrifice them all so that her faith would be naked, so that she would learn not to trust in anything but God. Deep in her soul, he laid the guidelines for progressive and finally perfect communication, effected in prayer and admitting no interruption of the interior dialogue between the soul and God: between God and the soul who must listen, and follow him. Jeanne Jugan's encounter with the spirituality of St. John Eudes, and the well-timed training in the Third Order, provided her with exactly those sure and balanced means for an intense and continuous inner life.

Thus God prepared this pure masterpiece, in which all Christian virtues come together. Not excluding the prime virtue of initiative, though hidden in that simple-hearted love and fundamental poverty in which all virtues are resolved, like the colours of a rainbow, into one brilliant, limpid light. Jeanne Jugan's work, all said and done, great though it was, is comparable to any other great human achievement. If we choose to go no further than to consider it at this level, it certainly does bear comparison — but other achievements are even more extensive and technically more advanced. The true greatness of her achievement is first that it is out of all proportion to the human means which brought it about; and secondly, that this work is still bathed in the radiance shining from its foundress's heart: her houses are like her, or rather they are like him whose hands built them by means of the foundress; they reflect the love of God.

To bring these institutions into existence and to set them on the road to success at a stroke, as it were, was doubly hard. First, because no work of this sort, if of purely human agency, can be built up in so short a period of time. Things have to be thought about, feasible plans have to be made, collaborators have to be found, finance and staff have to be slowly assembled, unavoidable administrative delays have to be allowed for. . . . But the Master Workman's methods are not these. God overrides things normally indispensable, or at least a great many of them. What money and endowments will not provide, faith has to provide instead. "Give, give the house. If God fills it, God will not forsake it."[1] Faith like this is put to the test every minute. Every minute, faith must triumph over appearances, must hope against every reason for losing hope, must courageously reach out for the hand of God, since he removes the human supports as we go, for us to make headway supported by him alone.

And thus the world map of charity grows gradually the richer for all these houses, potential inmates for which are never hard to find. The wind of the Spirit wafts the seeds across the oceans. Wherever they fall, they take root: so that one of the characteristics of this organization is the resolutely international atmosphere of the houses, be they where they may.

The story of each one of these foundations cries out to be recorded. Achievements of faith and love, each has an epic quality about it. And even if the best is never consigned to paper since already written in the soul, the facts are there to speak for themselves.

The miraculous fertility, you see, is first and foremost in the heart. The Little Sisters go on being what they are, aware that the best and only reason for their hope lies in fidelity to their ideal. . . . Jeanne Jugan's work goes on.

God's work goes on.

---

[1] cf. André Dupin's discourse to the Académie Francaise, 11 December, 1845.

CHRONOLOGY OF
THE LIFE OF JEANNE JUGAN
1792-1879

25 October, 1792   Birth of Jeanne Jugan, sixth child of Joseph Joucan* and Marie Horel in the hamlet of Petites-Croix, Cancale (Ille-et-Vilaine). She was baptized the same day by Monsieur Godefroy, the parish priest (a member of the constitutional clergy, having subscribed to the Civil Constitution of the Clergy on 12 July, 1790).

April 1796   Jeanne's father is lost at sea.

1801   Concordat between Church and State. Religious strife, particularly severe in western France, dies down. The church of St. Méen, Cancale, reopens for public worship.

1803   Cancale gets a new parish priest, the Rev. Alexis Met, formerly secretary to Msgr. de Pressigny, Bishop of the diocese of Saint-Malo which

---

*JOUCAN was her proper family name, but at Saint-Servan it became assimilated to JUGAN, which is a common surname in those parts, and in this form has gone down to posterity.

is henceforth by terms of the Concordat annexed to the diocese of Rennes. Presumed year of Jeanne's first communion.

1810   Jeanne receives a first proposal of marriage from a young sailor. She considers herself too young to make a binding decision and refuses him. About this time, she enters the service of the Vicomtesse de la Choüé as kitchen maid, at the Mettrie-aux-Chouettes, an estate in the village of Saint-Coulombe, three miles from Petites-Croix.

1816   Important mission at Cancale conducted by M. Gilbert and some twenty other priests. Jeanne attends the mission services. Her desire to give herself entirely to the Lord grows stronger, though she does not as yet know what form this giving should take.
The sailor who had proposed in 1810, proposed to her again. She refuses him definitely. To her family, who find her refusal hard to understand, she says: "God wants me for himself. He is reserving me for a work as yet unknown, for a work as yet unfounded."

1817   Jeanne is now twenty-five. Presumed date of her joining the Third Order of the Heart of the Admirable Mother, founded by St. John Eudes in the seventeenth-century. Jeanne finally leaves Cancale for Saint-Servan. She takes a job in a hospital (Hôpital du Rosais), founded in 1712 and run by the Daughters of Wisdom. She stays there for about six years, first as nurse to an aged and infirm priest, then as dispensary assistant.

1823   Exhausted, Jeanne leaves the hospital for the house of Mademoiselle Lecocq, near the church of Sainte-Croix, in Saint-Servan. She lives there for twelve years, more as companion than as maid. Together, the two women visit the poor and teach children the catechism.

1832   The Saint-Servan "charity office" helps 2,000 poor people. Five years later, the number has risen to 3,500.

1833   Arrival of the Hospitaller Brothers of St. John of God at Dinan-Lehon (Côtes-du-Nord).

1835   Mlle. Lecoq dies aged sixty-three, leaving Jeanne her furniture and savings, such as they are.

Summer 1835   Jeanne works part-time for well-to-do families in the neighbourhood, notably for M. Tréhouart de Beaulieu at La Goëletterie, 3 km from Saint-Servan, and for the Comte de Gouyon de Beaufort at Saint-Malo.

1837-38   Jeanne Jugan and Francoise Aubert, an older friend, rent a second-floor flat at No. 2, Rue du Centre, Saint-Servan. Francoise keeps house and Jeanne goes out nursing.

1838	M. Edouard Gouazon, a municipal councillor entrusts Jeanne with his seventeen-year-old ward, Virginie Trédaniel.
Winter 1839	Jeanne takes in Anne Haneau (born Chauvin), an aged, blind and infirm widow. A second old woman, Isabelle Coeuru, is taken in soon afterwards. Virginie Trédaniel and a friend of hers, Marie Jamet, help Jeanne at home in looking after these new inmates. Virginie and Marie are both Children of Mary and have had M. Le Pailleur, curate of Saint-Servan, as their confessor since 18 January, 1838.
15 October, 1840	At a meeting between Jeanne, Virginie, Marie and M. Le Pailleur, an association is formed and a rule adopted, based on that of the Third Order of the Heart of the Admirable Mother.
December 1840	A sick working-girl, Madeleine Bourges, comes to be looked after by Jeanne.
1 October, 1841	Jeanne and her companions move out of the flat in the Rue du Centre and take their old women to ground floor premises in the Rue de la Fontaine, where twelve old people can be accommodated.
Winter 1841-42	With the support and advice of the Brothers of St. John of God, and particularly of Fr. Félix Massot, Provincial Secretary of the Hospitaller Order, Jeanne institutes the collecting of alms.

2 February, 1842	Ever mounting demand for admission by old people. The former convent of the Daughters of the Cross is acquired for Jeanne by Mlle. Doynel, a well-to-do tradeswoman of Saint-Servan, and M. Le Pailleur, now officially entrusted with the work by the parish priest, M. Hay de Bonteville. Mlle. Doynel and M. Le Pailleur act as co-trustees of the new association. By collecting, Jeanne pays off the large debt in one year.
Spring 1842	The acquisition of new premises gives rise to local animosity. Representations are made to Msgr. Brossais Saint-Marc, Bishop of Rennes, who consults M. de Bonteville and then gives full support to Jeanne's activities.
29 May, 1842	Jeanne is unanimously elected superior of the little association, in the presence of M. Le Pailleur and Mlle. Doynel. Marie Jamet and Madeleine Bourges promise obedience to Jeanne. The association adopts the name "Servants of the Poor." A hospitaller rule is worked out, based on the rule of the Brothers of St. John of God.
10 July, 1842	Virginie Trédaniel, not present at the election, ratifies it and promises obedience to Jeanne.
15 August, 1842	Marie, Virginie and Madeleine take a simple vow of chastity for six months. Jeanne, as a tertiary of the

	Heart of the Admirable Mother, had already privately taken a perpetual vow of chastity.
29 August, 1842	Jeanne and her companions receive a diploma of "union of prayers and spiritual favours" from the Hospitaller Order of St. John of God. It bears the signature of Br. Benoit Verno, Prior General, countersigned by Fr. Paul de Magallon, Provincial of France, and Fr. Félix Massot, Provincial Secretary.
29 September, 1842	First visit of Msgr. Brossais Saint-Marc, Bishop of Rennes, to the ground floor premises in the Rue de la Fontaine.
29 September, 1842	Move to the former Convent of the Cross, renamed Maison de la Croix (House of the Cross). Virginie and Madeleine move in to look after the poor, of whom there are now eighteen.
15 October, 1842	Marie Jamet leaves home and moves into the House of the Cross.
20 October, 1842	She is appointed councillor to Jeanne, who teaches her how to go collecting.
21 November, 1842	Jeanne and Marie take a private vow of obedience for one year.
8 December, 1842	Virginie and Madeleine also take the vow of obedience. All four renew their vow of chastity.
Winter 1842-43	Jeanne takes in the first old man, Rodolphe Laisné, a former sailor, aged about seventy-five.

8 December, 1843	Jeanne is re-elected superior of the "Servants of the Poor."
23 December, 1843	M. Le Pailleur, on his own authority (as he later declares), quashes the election of 8 December, and chooses Marie Jamet, aged twenty-three, to replace Jeanne, aged fifty-one.
January 1844	Eulalie, Marie Jamet's younger sister, joins her at the House of the Cross, and is soon followed by Francoise Trévily, the daughter of an Erquy fisherman.
February 1844	The "Servants of the Poor" change their name to "Sisters of the Poor" and take names in religion: Jeanne becomes Sister Mary of the Cross, Marie becomes Sister Marie-Augustine of the Compassion, Virginie becomes Sister Marie-Thérèse of Jesus, Madeleine becomes Sister Marie-Joseph.
7 February, 1844	They take their first vows of poverty and hospitality for one year.
21 December, 1844	A memorandum describing the early stages of the work is drawn up for submission to the Académie Francaise, with a view to getting Jeanne awarded the Prix Montyon, a money prize "designed to reward a poor French man or woman for outstandingly meritorious activity." The memorandum is signed by M. Hay de Bonteville, parish priest of Saint-Servan, and fourteen members of the Town Council, countersigned by the Mayor,

	M. Douville, and M. Louis Blaire, representing the sub-prefect of Saint-Malo.
Autumn 1845	The Institut de France informs the Mayor of Saint-Servan that the Montyon Prize (first class) has been awarded to "Miss Jeanne Jugan" by the Académie Francaise.
11 December, 1845	The customary discourse on the award is pronounced at the annual public session of the Académie Francaise by M. André Dupin. Among those present are the most celebrated authors of the age: Chateaubriand, Lamartine, Victor Hugo, Thiers, Mérimée, Cousin, Mignet, Guizot, Sainte-Beuve. ...
December 1845- January 1846	The award of the Prix Montyon to Jeanne Jugan is widely reported in the national and local press.
19 January, 1846	Jeanne goes collecting in Rennes for the house at Saint-Servan. She realizes that a foundation is needed at Rennes too, and founds it the following month. Eulalie Jamet, now Sister Mary of the Conception, is appointed to be its superior.
4 August, 1846	Jeanne goes to Dinan where she founds a third house, which she provisionally accommodates in a bastion of the city walls. Eighteen days later, she is visited by an English tourist who later publishes a long article about her in the English press. Evidence suggests that this was the famous novelist Charles Dickens.

24 August, 1846	Jeanne buys the former Capuchin convent in Dinan for her new foundation there.
1846	The local press of Rennes and Dinan publish a number of articles praising her work.
January 1847	M. Dupont, known as "the holy man of Tours," asks Jeanne to found a house there. Sr. Marie-Augustine de la Compassion is deputed for the job.
December 1847	First General Chapter of the "Sisters of the Poor." Jeanne is not invited.
February 1848	Jeanne at Rennes.
April 1848	Jeanne urgently called to Dinan, to come to the rescue of the new foundation there.
13 September, 1848	Long article by Louis Veuillot on the front page of *L'Univers* on Jeanne Jugan's work and its right to public support.
Winter 1848	Mother House and Novitiate moved to Tours.
3 February, 1849	The Bishop of Saint-Brieuc endorses the work of Jeanne Jugan "well known for the institutions which she has founded."
10 February, 1849	Jeanne arrives in Tours, where her work is soon as fruitful as it has already been at Dinan.
1849	Foundations in Paris, Nantes and Besancon, this last at the request of Mlle. Junot who knows about Jeanne's work from reading *L'Univers*.

	About now, the popular name "Little Sisters of the Poor" is officially adopted by the Institute.
December 1849	Jeanne collects funds in Anjou.
1850	Foundations in Angers, Bordeaux, Rouen and Nancy. The Angers foundation is due to Jeanne; there, as in Brittany and Touraine, she works herself to the bone to support the house.
Winter 1850	Jeanne leaves Angers for Dinan.
December 1850	The number of Little Sisters (novices and postulants included) passes the hundred mark. Second General Chapter.
1851	Novitiate moved from Tours to Paris. First foundation in England.
May 1852	Formal approbation of the Institute by Msgr. Brossais Saint-Marc, Bishop of Rennes.
1852	Marie Jamet and Virginie Trédaniel pronounce perpetual vows. Jeanne is not allowed to do so until 1854. The Mother House and Novitiate return to Rennes. Recalled to and retained at the Mother House, Jeanne begins her long retirement there, among the novices and postulants.
June 1853	First foundation in Belgium.
December 1853	Jeanne becomes a member of the General Council, remaining so until June 1878: an appointment evidently meant to be honorary rather than effective; her presence in Council is only recorded on one occasion.

9 July, 1854	Approbation of the Institute by Pope Pius IX. The Congregation now numbers 500 Little Sisters and 36 houses.
8 December, 1854	Jeanne takes perpetual vows with Madeleine Bourges.
1855	At the request of the Guérin de la Grasserie family, Léon Brune paints Jeanne's portrait (without her knowing).
1856	Legal recognition of the Congregation by decree of Napoleon III.
30 January, 1856	Acquisition of the estate known as La Tour, in the village of Saint-Pern (Ille-et-Vilaine) Mother House and Novitiate move there at the beginning of April, Jeanne a little later. Final retirement for her, but also the beginning of a period incalculably rich in spiritually speaking. Sharing the life of the novices and postulants, the foundress impresses her own ideals on them.
20 March, 1857	Foundation stone of the Novitiate laid. The buildings are not completed until 1876.
1863	First foundation in Spain.
May 1866	The Municipality of Saint-Servan renames the street where the House of the Cross stands, in honour of Jeanne Jugan.
1867	Foundation of the Congregation's hundredth house: Toulon.
1868	First foundations in Ireland, America and North Africa.

1869	First foundation in Italy.
1878	Foundation in Malta.
1 March, 1879	Pope Leo XIII approves the constitutions of the Congregation, now numbering 2,400 Little Sisters, for a period of seven years.
29 August, 1879	Death of Jeanne Jugan (Sister Mary of the Cross), aged eighty-six, at the Tour Saint-Joseph.
10 July, 1970	Introduction of the cause of Jeanne Jugan by a decree of the Congregation for the Causes of Saints.

SELECT BIBLIOGRAPHY

A. Leroy, *History of the Little Sisters of the Poor*, Burns, Oates & Wasbourne, London, 1925.

Chanoine A. Helleu, *A Great Breton, Jeanne Jugan*, The Burleigh Press, Bristol, 1939.

Msgr. Francis Trochu, *Jeanne Jugan*, printed by F.A. Clements, Chatham, second revised edition, 1960.

Maria Winowska, *Pioneer of Unity*, Burns & Oates, London, 1969.

Little Sisters of the Poor, *Sayings of Jeanne Jugan*, printed by J. Lyons, Sydney, 1970, printed by the Daughters of St. Paul, Boston, Massachusetts, 1972.

JONAH:
Spirituality of a Runaway Prophet   1.75

Roman Ginn, o.c.s.o. While acquiring a new appreciation for this very human prophet, we come to see that his story is really our own. It reveals a God whose love is unwavering yet demanding, for if we are to experience the freedom of mature Christians, we must enter the darkness of the tomb with Christ, as Jonah did, in order to rise to new life.

POOR IN SPIRIT:
Awaiting All From God   1.75

Cardinal Garrone. Not a biography of the Mother Teresa of her age, this spiritual account of Jeanne Jugan's complete and joyful abandonment to God leads us to a vibrant understanding of spiritual and material poverty. This founder of the Little Sisters of the Poor left behind a life that is a spiritual classic, inspiring us in our search to live as the Lord would have us.

. . . AND I WILL FILL THIS HOUSE WITH GLORY:
Renewal Within a Suburban Parish   1.50

Rev. James A. Brassil. This book helps answer the questions: What is the Charismatic Renewal doing for the Church as a whole? and What is the prayer group doing for the parish? With a vibrant prayer life and a profound devotion to the Eucharist, this Long Island prayer group has successfully endured the growing pains inherent to the spiritual life, the fruit of which is offered to the reader.

DESERT SILENCE:
A Way of Prayer for an Unquiet Age   1.75

Rev. Alan J. Placa. The pioneering efforts of the men and women of the early church who went out into the desert to find union with the Lord has relevance for those of us today who are seeking the pure uncluttered desert place within to have it filled with the loving silence of God's presence.

Order from your bookstore or
LIVING FLAME PRESS, Locust Valley, N.Y. 11560

PRAYING WITH SCRIPTURE IN THE HOLY LAND:
Daily Meditations With the Risen Jesus
2.25

Msgr. David E. Rosage. Herein is offered a daily meeting with the Risen Jesus in those Holy Places which He sanctified by His human presence. Three hundred and sixty-five scripture texts are selected and blended with the pilgrimage experiences of the author, a retreat master, and well-known writer on prayer.

DISCOVERING PATHWAYS TO PRAYER
1.75

Msgr. David E. Rosage. Following Jesus was never meant to be dull, or worse, just duty-filled. Those who would aspire to a life of prayer and those who have already begun, will find this book amazingly thorough in its scripture-punctuated approach.

"A simple but profound book which explains the many ways and forms of prayer by which the person hungering for closer union with God may find him." **Emmnauel Spillane, O.C.S.O., Abbot, Our Lady of the Holy Trinity Abbey, Huntsville, Utah.**

REASONS FOR REJOICING
Experiences in Christian Hope
1.75

Rev. Kenneth J. Zanca. The author asks: "Do we really or rarely have a sense of excitement, mystery, and wonder in the presence of God?" His book offers a path to rejuvenation in Christian faith, hope, and love. It deals with prayer, forgiveness, worship and other religious experiences in a learned and penetrating, yet simple, non-technical manner. **Religion Teachers' Journal.**

"It is a refreshing Christian approach to the Good News, always emphasizing the love and mercy of God in our lives, and our response to that love in Christian hope." **Brother Patrick Hart, Secretary to the late Thomas Merton.**

CONTEMPLATIVE PRAYER:
Problems and An Approach for the Ordinary Christian
1.75

Rev. Alan J. Placa. This inspiring book covers much ground: the struggle of prayer, growth in familiarity with the Lord and the sharing process. In addition, he clearly outlines a method of contemplative prayer for small groups based on the belief that private communion with God is essential to, and must precede, shared prayer. The last chapter provides model prayers, taken from our Western heritage, for the enrichment of private prayer experience.

THE ONE WHO LISTENS:
A Book of Prayer
2.25

Rev. Michael Hollings and Etta Gullick. Here the Spirit speaks through men and women of the past (St. John of the Cross, Thomas More, Dietrich Bonhoeffer), and present (Michel Quoist, Mother Teresa, Malcolm Boyd). There are also prayers from men of other faiths such as Muhammed and Tagore. God meets us where we are and since men share in sorrow, joy and anxiety, *their* prayers are *our* prayers. This is a book that will be outworn, perhaps, but never outgrown.

ENFOLDED BY CHRIST:
An Encouragement to Pray
1.95

Rev. Michael Hollings. This book helps us toward giving our lives to God in prayer yet at the same time remaining totally available to our fellowman — a difficult but possible feat. Father's sharing of his own difficulties and his personal approach convince us that "if he can do it, we can." We find in the author a true spiritual guardian and friend.

PETALS OF PRAYER:
Creative Ways to Pray
1.50

Rev. Paul Sauvé. *"Petals of Prayer is an extremely practical book for anyone who desires to pray but has difficulty finding a method for so doing. At least 15 different methods of prayer are described and illustrated in simple, straightforward ways, showing they can be contemporary even though many of them enjoy a tradition of hundreds of years. In an excellent introductory chapter, Fr. Sauvé states that the best 'method' of prayer is the one which unites us to God. . . . Father Sauvé masterfully shows how traditional methods of prayer can be very much in tune with a renewed church."* **St. Anthony Messenger.**

Order from your bookstore or
LIVING FLAME PRESS, Locust Valley, N.Y. 11560

CRISIS OF FAITH:
Invitation to Christian Maturity
1.50

Rev. Thomas Keating, o.c.s.o. How to hear ourselves called to discipleship in the Gospels is Abbot Thomas' important and engrossing message. As Our Lord forms His disciples, and deals with His friends or with those who come asking for help in the Gospels, we can receive insights into the way He is forming or dealing with us in our day to day lives.

IN GOD'S PROVIDENCE:
The Birth of a Catholic Charismatic Parish
1.50

Rev. John Randall. The engrossing story of the now well-known Word of God Prayer Community in St. Patrick's Parish, Providence, Rhode Island, as it developed from Father Randall's first adverse reaction to the budding Charismatic Movement to today as it copes with the problems of being a truly pioneer Catholic Charismatic Parish.

"This splendid little volume bubbles over with joy and peace, with 'Spirit' and work." **The Priest.**

SOURCE OF LIFE:
The Eucharist and Christian Living
1.50

Rev. Rene Voillaume. A powerful testimony to the vital part the Eucharist plays in the life of a Christian. It is a product of a man for whom Christ in the Eucharist is nothing less than all.

SEEKING PURITY OF HEART:
The Gift of Ourselves to God
illus. 1.25

Joseph Breault. For those of us who feel that we do not live up to God's calling, that we have sin of whatever shade within our hearts. This book shows how we can begin a journey which will lead from our personal darkness to wholeness in Christ's light — a purity of heart. Clear, practical help is given us in the constant struggle to free ourselves from the deceptions that sin has planted along all avenues of our lives.

**Order from your bookstore or
LIVING FLAME PRESS, Locust Valley, N.Y. 11560**

PROMPTED BY THE SPIRIT

2.25

Rev. Paul Sauvé. A handbook by a Catholic Charismatic Renewal national leader for all seriously concerned about the future of the renewal and interested in finding answers to some of the problems that have surfaced in small or large prayer groups. It is a call to all Christians to find answers with the help of a wise Church tradition as transmitted by her ordained ministers. The author has also written *Petals of Prayer/Creative Ways to Pray*.

DISCOVERING PATHWAYS TO PRAYER

1.75

Msgr. David E. Rosage. Following Jesus was never meant to be dull, or worse, just duty-filled. Those who would aspire to a life of prayer and those who have already begun, will find this book amazingly thorough in its scripture-punctuated approach.

"A simple but profound book which explains the many ways and forms of prayer by which the person hungering for closer union with God may find him." **Emmanuel Spillane, O.C.S.O., Abbot, Our Lady of the Holy Trinity Abbey, Huntsville, Utah.**

THE BOOK OF REVELATION:
What Does It Really Say?

1.75

Rev. John Randall, S.T.D. The most discussed book of the Bible today is examined by a scripture expert in relation to much that has been published on the Truth. A simply written and revealing presentation.

Order from your bookstore or
LIVING FLAME PRESS, Locust Valley, N.Y. 11560

Books by Venard Polusney, O. Carm.

UNION WITH THE LORD IN PRAYER
Beyond Meditation To Affective Prayer Aspiration And Contemplation
.85

"A magnificent piece of work. It touches on all the essential points of Contemplative Prayer. Yet it brings such a sublime subject down to the level of comprehension of the 'man in the street,' and in such an encouraging way."
Abbott James Fox, O.C.S.O. (former superior of Thomas Merton at the Abbey of Gethsemani)

ATTAINING SPIRITUAL MATURITY FOR CONTEMPLATION (According to St. John of the Cross)
.85

"I heartily recommend this work with great joy that at last the sublime teachings of St. John of the Cross have been brought down to the understanding of the ordinary Christian without at the same time watering them down. For all (particularly for charismatic Christians) hungry for greater contemplation."
Rev. George A. Maloney, S.J., Editor of Diakonia, Professor of Patristics and Spirituality, Fordham University.

THE PRAYER OF LOVE . . . THE ART OF ASPIRATION
1.50

"It is the best book I have read which evokes the simple and loving response to remain in love with the Lover. To read it meditatively, to imbibe its message of love, is to have it touch your life and become part of what you are."
Mother Dorothy Guilbault, O. Carm., Superior General, Lacombe, La.

From the writings of John of St. Samson, O. Carm., mystic and charismatic

PRAYER, ASPIRATION AND CONTEMPLATION
Translated and edited by Venard Poslusney, O. Carm.   Paper 3.95

All who seek help in the exciting journey toward contemplation will find in these writings of John of St. Samson a compelling inspiration and support along with the practical guidance needed by those who travel the road of prayer.

LIVING FLAME PRESS
BOX 74, LOCUST VALLEY, N.Y. 11560

Quantity

_____ Jonah — 1.75

_____ Poor in Spirit — 1.75

_____ And I Will Fill This House With Glory — 1.50

_____ Desert Silence — 1.75

_____ Praying With Scripture in the Holy Land — 2.25

_____ Discovering Pathways to Prayer — 1.75

_____ Reasons for Rejoicing — 1.75

_____ Contemplative Prayer — 1.75

_____ The One Who Listens — 2.25

_____ Enfolded by Christ — 1.95

_____ Petals of Prayer — 1.50

_____ Crisis of Faith — 1.50

_____ In God's Providence — 1.50

_____ Source of Life — 1.50

_____ Seeking Purity of Heart — 1.25

_____ Prompted by the Spirit — 2.25

_____ Discovering Pathways to Prayer — 1.75

_____ The Book of Revelation — 1.75

_____ Union With the Lord in Prayer — .85

_____ Attaining Spiritual Maturity — .85

_____ The Prayer of Love — 1.50

_____ Prayer, Aspiration and Contemplation — 3.95

QUANTITY ORDER: DISCOUNT RATES

For convents, prayer groups, etc.: $10 to $25 = 10%;
$26 to $50 = 15%; over $50 = 20%.
Booksellers: 40%, 30 days net.

NAME _____

ADDRESS _____

CITY _____ STATE _____ ZIP _____

☐ *Payment enclosed. Kindly include $.50 postage and handling on
order up to $5.00. Above that, include 10% of total up to $20.
Then 7% of total. Thank you.*